Welcome

To

Earth School

Become an enlightened soul

One class—One lesson

One journey at a time

Catherine Adams

Advocate of the Soul

THE LIBRARY OF CONGRESS HAS CATALOGED THIS BOOK AS FOLLOWS:

Adams, Catherine.

Welcome to Earth School

2010913796

TXu 1—722—469

International Standard Book Number: 1-4538-2483-9

978-1-4538-2483-2

Printed in the United States of America

Author's contact information:
Catherine Adams
Welcome to Earth School
P.O. Box 833
Seymour, TN 37876

www.Welcometoearthschool.com

www.Welcometoearthschool@yahoo.com

This book is devoted with great love

to my daughter

Kristie Marie

Special Dedication

To

Devanee McCurdy

Though we spent but a short time together, I miss you in this world. You filled your family and friends with the glow of love and joy that lives in our hearts and gives strength to our souls. Congratulations, my friend, on a life well lived.

With Love and Gratitude

So often, our lives are touched in ways that seem insurmountable at the time, which prove to be a wonderful catalyst for transformation and blessings later. It is with great joy, love and gratitude that I acknowledge those blessings in my life:

Kim Hansen, you have my deepest gratitude for your astounding support, vision, and belief in the message of this book.

Alissa Lukara, Editor: Book Whisperer, Facilitator of Truth and beautiful soul. Your skills and guidance drew out the true message of this book. Thank you for your patience and willingness to help me articulate what is held in my soul.

Carole Davis, Finishing Editor: Thank you for joining me in this great adventure by polishing and shining this book. I am in awe of your willingness to devote your time and expertise.

Mike, I thank you for gifting me the time and space to flourish. I am so grateful for the long weekends, hours of listening, understanding and your patience.

Kristie, you are a rare and magnificent soul. Your creativity and love infuse this book. Thank you for inspiring me to be more.

Efran, my Sacred and Holy Guardian Angel,—my deepest gratitude for always standing with me.

Jacob, you are the funniest guy on the planet. No one makes me laugh harder. Your keen eye and brilliant mind as an editor, proofreader, and fact finder helped me create a better book. You are amazing.

Jaiden, your joy and many talents will take you to the stars. You are a beautiful Light. Thank you for shining in my life.

Berta, you are the angel who heals my heart. Thank you for showing me the possibilities of this gift. I am so grateful for being part of your life.

Carlye, I thank you for sharing your gift of Light and love. You are an amazing woman, facilitator of spirit and champion of the soul.

June, you never gave up on me. You believed that I could write this book, and so I did. Your friendship and motivation are invaluable to me.

Merri, beautiful Light in my life. I am so thankful for your guidance, loving clarity and support. You are a blessing.

Anisa, I am so grateful for your encouragement and sharing your delight in the gift of life.

Mr. Potthoff, forty years ago you encouraged me to use my voice. Thank you for being a true teacher.

Table of Contents

Introduction

Let's start at the beginning…

Earth is an entire planet dedicated to the education of your soul. The moment you were born here, you began your Earth School curriculum. Every day of your life, you attend Classes, participate in lessons and gain the opportunity to create new energy for the growth of your soul.

Welcome to Earth School presents you with a fresh perspective of your unique soul journey. We examine the source of life itself, how we came into Being and the purpose of our creation, including an intimate look at the essence that is the Creator. We address both the physical and the spiritual, nonphysical worlds to help you visualize the entire picture of your existence before, during and after your time in Earth School. We also incorporate tools to help you recognize distractions and illusions on your Earth School journey.

First and foremost, this book illustrates how everything that transpires in your life can be viewed as an opportunity to learn or teach. The lessons presented on the Earth Campus give us all the opportunity to grow as individuals and as a society. Part of that growth involves identifying your true self, releasing fear, gathering wisdom and enlightening your soul.

Embracing this awareness, your purpose on the Earth Campus gains more clarity. The purpose of life here is to become wiser than you are moment by moment—to experience life, develop as a result of your lessons, and become a sage and knowledgeable soul.

Most of you recognize that your soul is held within your physical body when you are on the Earth Campus.

However, this book adds to that knowing and explores what your soul has the power to do here. Because your soul was born of creative energy, you have the power to create on Earth. This gives you the capability to change yourself, your life and ultimately, our world. The manner in which you live your everyday life on the Earth Campus determines who you are and what you can become from the education you receive.

This book serves as:
- An instruction manual to help you take advantage of the options and stages of Earth School
- A guidebook for the soul regarding opportunities available in Earth School
- An Earth Campus orientation
- A tutorial on how to identify and use your gifts and talents to live your finest life
- Advice and tools on becoming an empowered soul
- A reminder of Angelic grace accessible on Earth
- An outline of what ensues after graduation in the afterlife

I believe the timing of this book parallels a worldwide need to refocus our energy in a new direction. Many of us have lost perspective about our purpose. As a result, we scramble to fix what has been broken for so long—our connection to spirit. However, our wounds have become too deep for temporary fixes. Our societies, environments, physical bodies, mental and emotional states, as well as hunger for clarity are in desperate need of our attention.

This redirection needs to be accomplished in order for us to continue to have the learning environment that Earth School provides. If we destroy our world, our souls will not have the same opportunity to experience and learn.

On my own journey to connect with spirit and find purpose, I have seen with my gift of clairvoyance the beauty of souls on the many levels of Light and souls down in the depths of darkness. I have stood in the abyss, surrounded by the stench of nothingness, and floated on the energy of The Creator.

The question I continually asked myself while experiencing my inner sight was, "How is this possible?" This is not what I was taught, believed or could have imagined. Nonetheless, it exists.

The information documented in this book has been gathered over the course of my lifetime. At the age of 22, I began to see Angels, spirits and places that were not visible to the physical eye, but only through my inner vision. Years later, after honing my skill through study and prayer, I began to work with people, more than five thousand to date, who came to me looking for direction. The gift I offered in our sessions was to see with the eyes of my soul, to work in the Light and advocate for their souls' highest good.

By asking The Creator permission to spiritually *see* a client, I was guided, step-by-step by the Light to assist others to receive healing and clarity. I met each client's Guardian Angel, who appeared to offer a stronger bond with the client and to help, guide and comfort. In the majority of sessions, healers, guides and souls that have crossed over, also appeared to give advice, moral support and love.

During the sessions and from information that came to me in my life experience and in meditation, I learned more about the journey of the soul and the movement of energy. I was repeatedly shown the material that now appears in this book.

You might wonder what authority is the source of the knowledge I have received. The answer is The Highest Light, Angels of every sort, Guides for the Journey, enlightened Advisors, Saints, and souls who have lived their truth and are sharing their wisdom.

Some of the people I have worked with over the years call me a medium. Others assume I am a psychic. Many say I am a healer or that I balance energy. The Highest Light calls me a messenger. But if I had to put a name on what I am, it would be an Advocate for the Soul. It is that aspect of the Light from which my soul was created.

The path of my life has been a voyage of personal transformation. My goal is to cultivate what is holy in the midst of my daily tasks and to transform my life with spiritual grace. My strong intention is to pursue a conscious awareness of Divinity and a communion with The Creator through my direct experience or insight. To be a Soul Advocate is to choose to embrace the highest good for all souls. In my life, I seek to become my true self, but I can only do this by letting go of who I am not.

My passion for our souls and the recognition that we are all connected is an integral part of my Being. This book stems from my desire to help all of us live as fully as possible, to encourage the world to be a better, more compassionate place and to help each other live mindfully.

Like you, I, too, am a soul who attends Earth School to practice my gifts, enhance my talents, and learn from my accomplishments, as well as my mistakes. However, decades of my education passed before I recognized that the spiritual path had been the calling of my soul.

Then for years, as I worked with people in sessions, they told me, "You must write a book. We all need to know what you have seen. Why don't we all know this? How could we have fixed this, if we didn't come to see you?"

Gradually, the call to write about what I have learned on my life path became an undeniable calling of my soul as well. And that is why I wrote this book—to answer that call and to share what I know to be true. My hope is that it will empower you to live from your soul using your own gifts and abilities while you attend Earth School, guide you through life on Campus, and remind you that we all have Angelic help.

My own life lessons on this life journey have not been mastered, nor always chosen with grace, but I do know we can all access a flow of information in the Universe that is full of wisdom and love. That knowledge and understanding has found its way to me and enhanced my existence more than I thought possible. My goal is to take the insight I learn in Earth School back to my Higher Self, the whole of my soul, where it can be the catalyst for the illumination of my Being.

Meanwhile, my intention in this book is to share with you the role Earth School plays in your plans and purpose as well as in the afterlife. I will also share my own and clients' stories as illustrations of our Earth School journey. I also encourage you to review the Glossary as you move through this book to define and clarify words and terms that might be new to you.

- May this book give you insight into what is, what has always been, and what will always be.

- May these stories offer you a greater understanding of your own soul growth.

- May this day inspire you to live mindfully with love, compassion and gratitude.

- May you be blessed with many opportunities from which to learn.

This is one of the most important moments in my life as today is the day you have invited me to share my story and what I have learned with you. I thank you for this gift of your time that is so precious and fleeting.

Catherine Adams

Promise

Of

Earth School

Together we will learn and grow

It is a wondrous day

Consider for a moment that you were born here on the Earth Campus for the purpose of learning—for the growth of your soul and that you began planning your soul and human curriculum before you were ever born.

In order to attend Earth School, your soul joined with a physical body. Having this body gives you the opportunity to encounter lessons and Classes, and to interact with others in physical, emotional, mental and spiritual ways you cannot do when you are in soul form. You can only gain some experiences and understanding as a soul by having a human encounter, living a human life.

You might have thought you are here to have life adventures and to live as fully as possible. But what if living as fully as possible means recognizing that every moment is an opportunity to learn for the purpose of illuminating your Being.

Life is a Gift
Of Time and Opportunity

In truth, life on the Earth Campus is comprised of many Classes and classrooms, offering you every life circumstance conceivable. You can choose to participate in their lessons and teachings or dismiss them. However, by choosing to live from the knowledge and understanding of who you are, why you are in School, and what your soul is hoping to attain, the reality of an eternity of purpose becomes part of your everyday life.

Earth School is also an environment where you create with your life. Human encounters add to your soul awareness and are expressed through human form and interaction. You can refine your perspective here and recognize that you are responsible for your life choices. The more you know this, the greater the possibility that you will grow more than you thought possible and live your life in a way that illuminates your soul.

All of us choose to attend Earth School, and the Classes you asked to take are part of your adventure. You might sign up for Classes in Compassion, Frustration, Joy, Complacency, Jealousy or Affection. They all have many facets to understand and will provide you with an opportunity to obtain knowledge. What you do with that opportunity is up to you.

You can use it to create a unique and positive experience to grow into your best possible self and add Light, wisdom and insight to your soul. Or, you can produce a negative situation that may add shadow or darkness to your soul. Most souls end up adding combinations—enlightenment, bitterness, positive action, or harmful reaction—so much to learn.

All souls have the opportunity to learn whether they come to Earth School to encounter complex ways of being or if they choose to remain on the levels of pure energy. The advantage of attending Earth School is your soul gets to experience lessons on Earth physically, emotionally, mentally and spiritually. As a soul, without a body, your learning capabilities are strictly from an energetic form. You can also be a spectator, watching the choices and actions of other souls and what is brought forth by their free will. Conversely, being the active soul lets you encounter firsthand the consequences of choice as you acquire knowledge and skill, and as you change and gain true understanding, in all of your aspects.

In fact, you have the opportunity to learn in one lifetime on the Earth Campus what could take eons of time if you remained in the state of pure energy without a body. For example, if souls, who were residing on the energetic levels, wanted to learn all about love, they could talk to other souls who had insight to share on that subject. They could attain information by watching other souls, as well as Students on the Earth Campus, or review the accounts of love stored in the Universal Akashic Records, where all information is documented. They would spend a long time gaining complete wisdom in the subject of Love. If, in the future, they were asked what Love was, they would stop to recall what they had studied and learned about Love.

However, when you go to Earth School, you learn firsthand about love. The lessons and Classes in that subject are innumerable. You can be the recipient, the giver, the caretaker or the teacher of love. You experience firsthand being emotionally in love, mentally in love, physically in love and spiritually in love. You can be in love with peace or chaos. You can embrace toxic love, the fullness of love or the void of love. You can experience what takes place within you when love is lost or leaves. You can explore unrequited love, unwanted love, the love of a child, a lover, the love of friendship, family love, and the unbridled love of a pet. You can love a place or time, things of sentiment or wealth.

Through those experiences, the meaning of Love becomes innately yours. You would not hesitate or need to stop to recall what Love is and what it means. You understand. You have lived it. Love is part of you.

Your time in Earth School is not the whole of your existence, but rather a small part of your soul journey. It begins with the birth of the body and ends with the death of the body. Your soul journey begins with the creation of your soul and never ends.

Your soul was not created to live in human form for one lifetime, after which you would be judged for your actions and spend eternity in Light or cast way in darkness. Our souls spring from the Light to exist for an eternity. You have as much time as necessary to learn, guide, create, love, forgive, nurture and foster new energy and ideas, so that you can become more than you are now—better, wiser, more joyful, abundant and ever growing.

As a Student on the Earth Campus you face many challenges as you tackle the curriculum you have chosen for yourself. Some lives are full of surprises, twists and turns, while others can tread along a slow and plodding path. Each soul's experience is different, but our life stories will have commonalities and diversities. Earth is not always an easy place to be. That is why it is such an excellent place to learn.

Your path through Earth School will be different from mine, but our goal may be the same. Some journeys through life's learning potential scale mountains. Others are a collection of rambling roads. You take Main Street, and I will take First Street, which is longer, but the difference would be our choice. In the end, we might still arrive at the same destination, or at least intend to.

The meaning of life might seem complicated, but do not be fooled. It is not a mystery.

The actual purpose of life is to create.

Every moment, you generate energy with your thoughts, actions, intentions, words and expressions. Consider for a moment: What is your objective and what will you create with your life? What you intend to create and what you actually do create may be two different things. Distractions of the physical world and pressure from other souls might lead you down an alternate path. That is a lesson in itself. Will you let that happen? What will come of it? Is the result what you envisioned? My best advice is to live in your truth.

As each choice is made in Earth School, a thought is formed, and an action is carried out, the sequence of those events affects the flow of Earth's energy. In essence, you not only attend Earth School in human form, but you and every other Student also impact the School environment. As a result, this School becomes your collective living

13

creation—an environment that alters and shifts as it responds to what its Students create, as well as to its own force.

You have already taken your first step toward higher learning by choosing to be on the Earth Campus. Most of you prepared for this opportunity by electing to live in a place where many lessons and teachings are available to you. A few of you chose to come here for the experience, with no particular Classes in mind. Have you decided to gather wisdom or spread tyranny as part of learning? Please remember, you can always change your objective.

Our soul is miraculous energy that lives in all of us. When we discover our soul, our true essence, we learn that God is here in this world right now. Everything we encounter throughout the day is a spiritual opportunity. Every moment challenges us to rise to our highest, to choose strength over weakness, wisdom over ignorance, and love over fear. Every soul holds the awareness there is a greater power that loves us, that we yearn for, and that we seek to discover within ourselves.

Most of all, attending Earth School holds the promise of possibility. No one can take the journey to enlightenment for anyone else. It must be discovered and experienced individually. The path to Light and beauty is as important as that destination. As you pursue knowledge and wisdom, your education on the Earth Campus offers you the opportunity to add enlightenment to your spirit and illumination to your soul.

The Birth of a Soul

Unlimited Possibilities

Many people have asked me how our souls came into Being. Were we all created at the same time? Are there old souls and new souls? Why are we different, but still the same? Why do our souls join with a physical body and come to Earth School? Do we choose our parents or the amount of time we have on Earth? Do we come here more than once?

Before I spoke to other people about these matters, it was necessary for me to fully comprehend and be enlightened about them myself. So, I asked for more insight. Many answers came in bits and pieces, but sometimes I received unexpected knowledge. That was the case when I asked to be shown my own creation. The event was not revealed to me right away or all at one time.

Initially, I started seeing other souls in the moment of their creation, as if I were watching a movie where I sat separate, but felt connected to their experience. One day in 2002, simply by blinking, I saw a brilliant Light with the type of sparks you see from firework sparklers, dancing away from the central Light—stunningly brilliant. I went into a quiet room in my house, closed my eyes, and the story of my creation was shown to me by The Highest Light. I knew it to be true, because I had lived it. The knowledge of this treasured memory was inside of me. This is what I was shown:

CREATION. My first memory was an awareness of conscious thought and separateness. I was a spark of Light, who had burst forth from the Creator's brilliant energy, just as we all did. That glimmer was my soul at its very beginning. I felt whole and vibrant, but at the same time, somewhat small. My soul name is Anor.

There were other souls around me. I could tell they were in different stages of existence, as no two were the same. Some shone brightly, and others were a blend of Light and shadow. I saw luminous souls and those that were a single sparkle. Each soul was a different size.

All souls inherently hold the wisdom of our experiences and what we create with those encounters. This produces the differences that cause our soul Light to grow, subsist or dim. The dim or stained souls were those that had chosen darkness to add to their energy. I learned that you can add negativity to your soul, whether you are in Earth School or existing on a level of energy.

I also intrinsically knew that each soul sprang from different parts of the Creator's energy—the many expressions of God. My spark of the Creator's energy, my soul itself, and my greatest gift was the knowledge that every soul has a unique purpose. That is the aspect of the Creator from which I was born. As such, my soul energy strives to live in a way, act in a way, or speak in a way that expresses that knowledge that we are here for a reason, and our souls will live on for eternity.

Other souls around me sprang from the other parts of the Creator—such as the Healing, Protective, Creative, or Educator aspects. They held their own wisdom. The luminous Light some souls shone was so wondrous and inviting to me that I yearned to become more than a glimmer myself. I chose to discover what I could do to grow as others had.

All souls are aware of a place, a School, just beyond the levels of pure energy. The One that we were all born of created that School for souls that desired to grow and add their energy to the flow and illumination of the Universe. This School afforded the opportunity to learn in one lifetime what could take me eons of time to learn if I remained pure soul energy. This Campus is called Earth School, and going there became my intention.

Many times, I sent part of my soul, which then became my astral soul, to Earth School. Each lifetime, I choose different subjects to learn and various locations to experience. On some occasions, I chose to be male to enhance my opportunities and on other occasions, being female afforded the best prospects.

When I returned to pure soul energy after each lifetime, I spent time integrating what my astral soul brought back into my Higher Self. Each moment was carefully documented in my soul library, called my Akashic Records. By having records for each soul, nothing is lost, forgotten or discarded unless you do it with intent. We all have the opportunity to record what we have gathered in the Universal Akashic Records, where every soul has the chance to review what other souls have learned.

Wanting to know more, that same year I asked to spiritually view another part of my soul journey and was shown my most recent experience on the Earth Campus. This is what I witnessed:

1935. Before coming into a lifetime in Earth School that preceded my present one, I chose the Classes of Motherhood, Patience and Abandonment. I felt those subjects were the natural progression for my soul education. Even though I was advised by enlightened souls not to take Patience and Motherhood at the same time, I was more enthusiastic than careful, and in my opinion, thought the combination would make the most of my Earth School time. Now, I wish I had taken their advice.

Next, I selected a destination and life circumstance that would give me the greatest chance to experience my chosen subjects. My options for family and location appeared innumerable. I could join a large farming family in the Midwest, a young couple who were part of elite society in New York City, or a community in a small village on the Eastern seaboard, whose inhabitants survived as fishermen.

In the end, my decision was clear. I already knew where I wanted to be. One woman, named Catherine, had been very kind to me before she left for Earth School, and our souls were connected in a special way. I missed her very much and wanted to be part of her physical world.

On the Earth Campus, Catherine had become a wife to Patrick, the mother of seven children, and a devout Irish Catholic woman. As a soul, I became determined to be born as her child, thinking that in this way, we would be connected for a lifetime.

When Catherine became pregnant for the eighth time, I sent my soul energy into the fetus. However, this choice did not fit into the plan of the Universe and was not in the highest good for either of our souls. Using my free will, I put what I wanted before the needs of my soul and tried anyway. To my dismay, I was stillborn. Choices and consequences are part of every soul's journey.

Not having a viable body, my soul energy returned to the levels of Light. My education in Earth School was experienced as a soul held in an unborn baby. I learned about the pain a mother experiences when she loses a child. When Catherine handed me back to the Angels, I felt abandoned and struggled with patience in planning my time in Earth School. I was able to add some enlightenment to my Higher Self, the whole of my soul.

After that difficult encounter, I stayed on the energy levels for 19 years, working with other souls that stood in the Light. I became more practiced in the interaction and support of the society that is the Unity of Souls. I watched people on the Earth Campus and tried to study their mistakes and achievements. I learned to send loving energy to souls in Earth School that wanted extra support.

1953. Twenty years later, I tried to come to Catherine again, albeit indirectly. One of her single daughters, Susan, became pregnant. I believed that if I came to Earth through her, Susan would have to work to support us, and Catherine would most likely care for me. What I didn't plan for was Susan giving me up for adoption, without ever telling her mother she was pregnant. Catherine was not even aware of my existence. My soul had to adjust to my new circumstances. My selected lessons in Motherhood and Abandonment had already begun.

1954. I was adopted by a middle class couple in "The City of Angels"—Los Angeles, California. In a twist of fate, or by synchronicity, my adoptive parents named me Catherine.

I thought I could learn a great deal from my new family. A son had joined them two years prior to my arrival, and as I was woven into the family, my presence presented another learning equation for them. My new energy, personality, needs and wants co-mingled with their already established unit, testing their limits and boundaries as well as my own.

You never know when the Universe is listening and taking you seriously. As I look back on my life, I can see when my appeals were heard and answered.

1969. A defining moment in my life came in July 1969, when I was 13 years old. I had attended funerals before, but this one was for my father—the man who had adopted me, loved me and raised me as his own. My emotions were raw, ranging from the gut wrenching to the ridiculous. One moment, I grasped for breath and sobbed. The next, I watched the Pall Bearers carry the coffin from the altar to the hearse, and found it ironic and silly that my father's name was Paul. I laughed until I had to sit down. A few breaths later, I plunged back into crying a shower of tears that drenched the front of my first black dress, bought especially for the funeral.

I didn't realize at the time, but this experience involved all of my chosen Classes. I felt abandoned by my father and struggled to have patience to allow myself to heal and discover where my life would take me next. My lessons in motherhood now included the experience of my adoptive mother trying to be both mother and father to me.

This loss hurt beyond reason. I pleaded with God to *know* that my father lived on, that he was out of pain and that his soul was thriving. Why could nobody on Earth confirm this for me? I felt that if another person could tell me things that only my father and I knew, I would know he was speaking through that person to me and that he lived on. Certainly God would not want anyone to suffer this deeply without offering the comfort of this kind of knowledge.

"Please God, I pleaded, please, give someone the gift to do this." I did not know it at the time, but the Universe was listening.

Nine years passed.

1976. By the time I was 21 years old, I had given birth to my own child, which brought more lessons in my chosen subject of Motherhood. One night, I woke up, completely aware, sat up in bed and saw the figure of a small boy in the hallway, just outside of my bedroom. His predominant feature was a mischievous grin.

My heart began to pound. He was as close to my daughter's bedroom door as he was mine. He laughed—the kind of belly laugh that only children are capable of, and ran towards me. Just before he reached me, his body turned into fine white granules and swirled up through the ceiling. His presence scared me so much I didn't sleep the rest of the night. Over the next year, the scenario repeated five or six times, always leaving me trembling.

This was my first major glimpse into my clairvoyant ability. I had uncovered the ability to see souls that were on another dimension. I was seeing with my physical eyes and at the same time, seeing another dimension layered on the physical.

Years later, I came to realize that my clairvoyant ability was not one of my courses, but a gift that added another dimension to my existence and my Earth School experience. However, initially, I was afraid of what I did not understand and dreaded the thought of seeing the boy again. All I had heard about ghosts and haunted places amplified my fear. I also questioned if the boy was a creation of my imagination.

This notion was dispelled when one day, I found my brother sitting on the couch, looking pale. He told me he had been standing in my kitchen, when he saw a young boy in the hallway. Thinking the boy was a neighbor who had come to play with my child, he approached the boy and said, "She is not here, so you should go home." The boy laughed, transformed into fine white granules and vanished.

I had not shared my visions with anyone, yet now my brother, too, described the boy just as I had seen him. His experience confirmed to me that I was seeing another realm.

Then, I began to wonder, if I could see the spirit of a boy, could I see other places like the Golden City of Light, or maybe even God? Was it also possible to see my father, Angels, Guides or Saints? The possibilities were endless. The reality of what this gift could offer helped me overcome my fears. That was the moment I began my journey in search of tools to use my clairvoyant gift in the best way possible.

For the next few years, souls recognized me as a person who could see or discern them. Some call it being an open channel, without boundaries, control or understanding. Being woken up in the middle of the night by someone standing next to my bed became the norm. These encounters were frightening. My clairvoyance was so clear I could not tell if the figure was a real person or the energy of a soul who appeared as a person. Because the experiences happened so often, I can honestly say that if someone had broken into my house and touched my shoulder to wake me up, I would have looked at them said, "Not now," and gone back to sleep.

This was the beginning of realizing my gifts, talents and ultimately, my spiritual calling and path. Altogether, my Earth School education involved many aspects of soul growth.

1977. The next year, after many years of searching, I found my biological family. They lived 3,000 miles away. As fate would have it, the first information I uncovered was Catherine's phone number. Her soul name and earthly name were the same. I did not yet consciously know of my soul connection to her. Still I ached to meet her.

As far as I knew, she did not know about me, so I protected my biological mother's privacy. I held the belief that I didn't have the right to meet Catherine or even let her know she was my grandmother without Susan's permission. With a pounding heart, I made up a story to get my mother's phone number from her. Our short conversation touched me deeply. She ended it with, "God love ya."

Lying to my grandmother felt terrible, but I was happy to make contact with my birth mother. At first, Susan denied me, but then agreed to a distant, private relationship. I did not know then, but I was subconsciously fulfilling an energetic contract Susan and I had entered into—to be silent in exchange for life.

1978—1993. From the time I was 23 years old until I was 39, I began to see more and more souls who had crossed over. My first glimpse at another dimension had felt like unwrapping a gift that contained fascinating photographs, taken in the most sacred of places, but I still did not fully understand what was being shown to me. Afterwards, I yearned to learn everything I could about the pictures in order to discover the depth of the gift and all it contained.

My sincere desire to help the souls I saw led me to read books on the subject, seek out teachers, and practice being silent, so I could receive guidance from the Light. I aligned myself with God by connecting my soul straight up to the Creator, rather than dispersing it out in the direction of the distractions in School.

I asked for help for all the souls who found their way to me. Word seemed to get out on the other side that I was able to see and communicate with them. Some of them began to ask me to pass messages on to loved ones who were still on the Earth Campus. I asked The Light for help and was told I did not have to seek them out—simply to help those people who asked for my assistance. I told the souls on the other side they would have to influence people with whom they wanted to communicate to come to me. A few times, my doorbell rang, and the person standing at the door looked bewildered. The individual would say, "I have heard you are a Medium, but I don't know why I'm here. I just know I need to be." I knew then a soul on the other side had initiated the visit. My family and friends would also encourage the people they cared about to see me when they thought it would help them. That was so precious to me, knowing they were entrusting me with ones they loved.

During these years, my courses in Motherhood, Patience and Abandonment also continued in full swing. In addition to raising my daughter, I became a stepmother to six children in all.

1994. A significant turning point came when I entered my forties. My health was declining, and my naturopath suggested I should meet a counselor in my area named Carlye. At the time I didn't know this amazing, wise woman was about to help me change my life. The answers I had appealed for at my father's funeral began to unfold. She became my facilitator of healing and provided a safe place to just be. Carlye encouraged me to discover my true self and to embrace my gifts. She also supported me in learning to divert darkness, to shed the old layers covering my authentic self, and to *Just Ask* when I was ready for an answer. I am so grateful.

With her support, I became more adept at consciously seeing, communicating with, hearing and sensing souls that had crossed over. I learned to tune in and as importantly, I learned to shut off. Although I came to Earth School to learn my chosen subjects, I realized I had also come to hone my gifts of spirit and to honor the source of my soul energy. I grew into myself and followed my calling— to be an Advocate of the Soul.

At this time, I was living in Yreka, California. As I began to do sessions for other people, I saw past lives for many of my clients. I had known of my previous attempt at life in 1935, but asked to be more enlightened in this area. I was told by Guides in the highest Light, that many people in Earth School believe we are created by God, who then sends us to Earth. When He says so, we return to Him, and our life is reviewed. If He is displeased with us, He will cast us away forever.

What I was shown instead is that we are created *from* The Light. We are given free will, eternal love and the power to create. The Creator tells us to take as much time as we want, try life in a body as many times as we desire, and if we choose, come back and share our experiences.

I had felt afraid of what I saw with my inner vision and of the experiences my gifts brought me until I found the strength and courage to walk through fear and became brave. I became unwavering when I encountered shadow and darkness until I found peace. I knew nothing I saw with my inner vision could cause me harm, unless I allowed it. I began to use my clairvoyance as the gift it truly was. I became empowered spiritually and as an advocate for other souls.

I learned that energy in the Light had no reason to bother me or to try to frighten me. Only those in the shadow or darkness would attempt to do that. With strength and conviction, I demanded only those that stood with God were allowed around me. I demanded that those of shadow and darkness must leave, and they did. Sometimes they would try to return. However, I persisted and learned not to be the first one to back down—*ever*—because it empowers them.

Dealing with the energies of shadow and darkness, I discovered, is not unlike dealing with prank phone calls. Giving them a reaction allows them to feel like they are in control, and they keep calling. However, if you refuse to answer the phone, they become bored and move on.

Just as I had learned to protect myself from harm in the physical world growing up, now I ascertained how to protect my emotions, mental state and soul Light in the same way. I became skilled at drawing the line when evil approached on any level. I was not willing to be distracted by an unkind word, a lie told behind my back, or an attack on my spirituality. I drew boundaries on all levels and did my best to stop those in the spirit and physical realms that would step over them inappropriately.

I discovered the energy of people, places and things, as well as spiritual energy, had the potential to color my energy. I decided what and who to allow in my home, in my life and around my soul. My intention became to interact with people or circumstances that improved all the parts of me and added stronger positive energy. My goal was to become an enlightened soul.

1995. The time had come to reveal myself to my biological family. Family medical history was my driving force. Susan had already informed some of her siblings. Now, the whole family knew. My daughter and I were warmly welcomed and invited to our first family reunion, where we met more than sixty relatives. During that remarkable week, I found myself sitting at the family table surrounded by my aunts—five of Catherine's daughters.

They didn't know of my gift of clairvoyance, nor of my connection to their mother. But my youngest aunt began to tell this story about my grandmother, Catherine.

One day, Catherine told her the story of a baby daughter about whom she had never spoken. It started when a neighbor invited the women of the community, including Catherine, for lunch, to what was expected to be a simple gathering. Instead, she was introduced to a woman who claimed to have psychic abilities, and proceeded to tell Catherine that she saw three men in tuxedos standing around a wooden box in her future. The men looked troubled. She thought the prediction was ridiculous. She had never even seen one man in a tuxedo, let alone three. Besides, as a devout Catholic, she did not believe in psychics or fortune-telling. She believed you kept your problems to yourself, offered up your suffering and did the best you could.

A short time later, Catherine became pregnant with her eighth child. When she went into labor, her husband, Patrick, dropped her off at the hospital as was customary in those days. Her first seven children had been born after several hours of labor—but not this time.

One day passed, then two. On the third day, Patrick came to visit her. She reached up to him, pulled him close, and told him that if he did not get the doctor to come help her immediately, she did not think she would live. Patrick ordered the nurses to call the doctor.

The head nurse refused to disturb the doctor who was attending a formal medical function, but Patrick sent a messenger to fetch him anyway. Catherine's doctor asked two other physicians present at the event to assist him. All three of them, dressed in their tuxedos, rushed to Catherine's hospital bedside. Before they reached her, she lost consciousness.

Catherine told my aunt she remembered rising up out of her body. She was holding her baby in her arms, wrapped in a blanket of Light. She rose higher and higher. Then, Angels approached and encouraged her to go back—it wasn't her time. They had come for the baby.

The next thing Catherine knew she was back in her body in her hospital room. When she opened her eyes, she saw three doctors, dressed in tuxedos, gathered around a small box that held her stillborn daughter.

Patrick and Catherine named their little girl, Catherine, and buried her in the church cemetery.

My soul-body partnership has so far lasted 57 years, and I have traveled many roads. On this journey, I have realized my gift of connecting to spirit could be explored, ignored, used for good or evil, and any combination in-between. It was my choice, just as it is for all of us. My intention is to learn from my opportunities. After graduation, when my body expires, I hope to have gained wisdom that can be added to my soul Light.

This is my piece of the Universe, my part of the Creator, and my life experience in Earth School. This is what I have been shown and know to be true. The knowledge gained through thousands of sessions is what I offer you today. I invite you to join me as we examine the Universe and what part we all play in its evolution.

The Creator

There is logic …

There is reason …

And then there is the truth

What you call the Creator will not matter

What you do in the name of the Creator will matter

What you create will matter

If you create nothing, it will matter

I will always remember when God appeared to me in a manner that I could understand. It happened late one night as I prepared for bed. I found myself in the presence of Light. His face was aged and deeply lined, yet His eyes were clear and twinkling, like those of a young child. Pure white hair flowed all around Him from His head to beneath His chin. Gently swaying, each strand seemed to have its own breath.

I immediately questioned Him, as I always do when I see anyone with my clairvoyance. I stood strong and said, "Are you in the Light? If not, then you must go." He looked a little surprised and replied, "I Am The Light." It was then that He told me a few of His many names.

I Am God—Creator of the Universe—Chi—

Jesu——I Am—Elijah—Never Ending—

Mohammed—Ismael—Hosanna—Creator of Soul

Grand Orator—Earth's Energy—Goddess——

All That Shines—The Light—The Holiness—

Dove of Peace—The Culmination of Power and

Light—The True Healer—The Shepherd—Shrine

of Light—The Father—The Son—The Holy

Ghost—Buddha—Inner Light—Lamb of God—

Hismanal—All That Is—Higher Power—The Compassionate Heart—The Peacemaker—The Great Spirit—Heart of Hearts—Omni Present—Speaker of Truth—The Oneness

Then I heard a sound resembling whales singing, or perhaps it was more like chimes ringing. As I focused closely to discover the sound's origin, I was drawn to what appeared to be a tiny jewel clinging to a single strand of His hair. It was a stunning, brilliant ruby that refracted Light from every possible angle. It was a soul. The sound of pure joy was coming from that single soul.

Then I saw numerous jewels on countless hairs, each emanating their own jubilant sound. From the deepest amethyst to the softest amber, each one had a unique size and shape. The smallest, which seemed to be the soul of a child, shown as a blend of diamond and sapphire. Each soul had added their luminosity and vibration to the energy of God. All the sounds of the souls resounded in a harmony of tones.

I gazed in amazement as a strand of His beard floated towards me. Wrapping my arms and legs around it, I immersed my entire Being in it. I felt …. pure peace. My soul was whole and happy. But the second I began to fear that the immersion would stop, I was gently put down. I discovered that fear is negative energy and cannot co-exist with pure Light. Interestingly, on Earth, scientists have identified a sound at the edge of the Universe. They say it sounds like whales singing and chimes ringing.

Various cultures that live and study together on the Earth Campus see the Creator in different ways. Some see The Sacred Light in the elements of the Earth such as water, fire, rock and sky. Others experience God in a building with a designated leader, who proclaims to speak the word of The Great Spirit. A number of people see the Light in charitable works, like feeding the hungry and helping the homeless.

Many Students live centered in the love of Light, and their lives reflect gratitude for all that is. It gives them balance and purpose that they share with others. Scores of people look for God in ancient scriptures in tales of elders who documented their truths. More than a few question the existence of Pure Oneness, and some do not believe in a Higher Power.

Certain cultures believe The Inner Light has only one name and dismiss what is not known to them. Countless Students realize that the Higher Power is in every place, breath and word. It is the Universal energy of The Creator that takes numerous names and forms. Your recognition of The Light will be unique to your own personal relationship with The Oneness.

Over the centuries, this simple concept and definition of the Great One has been debated and fought over. Belief has become an area with little tolerance for differences. Some Students have taken it upon themselves to judge and persecute those of different beliefs. Wars have been waged, people hurt and killed over a name. However, The Great

Spirit has no place for hatred or judgment, as He is purely loving, kind and compassionate.

Whoever God is to you, the Creator is not *out there*. He is quietly inside of us. We are fashioned from the essence of Light. If the outer facade of the body fell away, and we felt and experienced from our true self, the connection of our souls, our Oneness, would be seen, felt, and known by all.

Your soul is a Spark of the Creator, and He breathes life and Light into it. You infuse color and energy to enhance its growth into what it will become because of your intentions and actions. You cut, polish and shine your soul in the best possible ways to perfect your Being. Your soul then illuminates with all the radiance you create.

What does the Creator look like?

He looks like love

... wind

... sound

... and peace.

He looks like you and me,

As He is the essence of us all.

Ten years ago, a mother and her 20 year-old-son, Trey, came to see me. He was looking for some direction in life. Together, we met his Angel, talked about his soul energy, his gifts and tools, and the Classes he hoped to experience in Earth School.

The Angel showed me that Trey had been adopted at birth. She warned him about a bone condition that was prevalent in his biological family. Both Trey and his mother told me that doctors had tried in vain to find a diagnosis for his pain.

In the distance, I saw a group of people walking up to us from the other side. They were dressed in traditional black clothing that symbolized they were a Hasidic Jewish family. The man who led the family was carrying a large leather book. When he came closer, I was able to tell it was the Talmud.

These souls were members of Trey's biological family. Some of them had carried the gene of the same bone disease when they were in the body on the Earth Campus. They were able to give information that helped him attend to his medical problem.

When our talk was coming to an end, and the older man turned to walk away, I asked him if he would explain to me why he still carried a Jewish holy book. He smiled, pointed upward and said, "Ah, there are many paths to the same goal."

...*And so it was that people searched for themselves by looking into the eyes of others and reached for a sense of self in the arms of another, and still they did not find it. They continued to reach out for the answer to their Being beneath rocks and on the banks of the rivers. They searched on golf courses and in skyscrapers, and still they did not find what they were seeking. They persisted by rummaging through books and schools, traversing bridges, and exploring the landscape of the Earth, and still they felt empty.*

...*And when they had tired, their minds became quiet, and their hearts were silent, their soul made itself known. In that moment, they discovered their true self by turning within. They found the Light held deep inside and began to live with the contentment of what they had discovered. They learned the simple truth that they had carried it with them all along.*

At this point, you might be wondering if it is possible for you to join with the Divine, to blend into that pure, positive, radiant energy. The answer is yes.

- When you are at perfect peace with yourself

- When you feel no anger or revenge

- When you bless the ones who have hurt you

- When you have no fear

- That is when it happens…and only then

You cannot stand with the Light of God and still hold negative energy. It would not add illumination, but cast shadows, and that is not possible. This is why you go to Earth School—to create with your life, face your fears and perfect your soul. That is why your life is a journey. You start at the beginning and create your life, one-step at a time. You decide which paths take you forward, backward or sideways, or you can choose to remain stationary. I hope you discover your truth and stand strong in that certainty. Although we get many chances in one lifetime to learn, the

Creator does not limit our possibilities to one life. We are loved too much to be told, "You are done, and you have no more opportunities."

Those who are ashamed of their actions, thoughts or deeds may move away from the Light. They can continue to go that way or move back towards pure, radiant energy.

Individuals who are negative are not comfortable in the vibration of Light, just as those who are positive do not feel at ease in darkness. But remember, we all came from the Light, even those who are now in the darkest of places.

Is it possible to rid yourself of the essence of Light? Some souls relish negativity and hatred. When they have added all the darkness and shadow they can to their soul, and that one spark of Light is left, they can throw it away with intent and become completely dark.

However, even then, that spark of Light is held for them in a place far away from where they dwell. At any time, they can ask for it to be returned to them. From that Spark, they are capable of moving out of the darkness to build a soul of Light with positive thoughts, words, and actions. Every soul is precious. None is thrown away. It is never too late to begin a journey back to the Light. The Universe is ever patient and imparts, "Please come home, my child. I love you. I will wait forever, but the choice needs to be yours."

Take a moment now to be silent and listen to what is always there for us—the words of the Creator:

"I created a society that is made up of every gift and ability. If your gift is to bake and your neighbor's gift is to build, bake for the fruit grower, the teacher and the priest, and they in turn will share what they have to offer.

"I formed a balanced society, but society becomes unbalanced when separation becomes prevalent. You are not separate and represent the whole of Light and goodness. Isolation can create fear. In coming together, the zest for life is shared and encouraged.

"Don't underestimate people. Every day, they step up to their challenges with the best of intentions. They are working to resolve their issues and to make the most of their learning opportunities.

"If you glanced inside of most homes, you would see kindness, love, appreciation, value and concern for each other.

"For every one driver who cut in front of you today, there were 100 who didn't. Which one will you remember? Do not ignore the quiet kindness

that happens every second of every minute of every day.

"The world contains more decency than evil. This quieter energy spreads peacefully. Seek it out, and be part of it.

"People are a blend of Light, shadow and darkness. Encourage the Light. Decide how you will deal with all the subtle shades and move forward in the best way possible.

"Speak freely and openly to each other. Show your weaknesses and strengths without shame and with determination to grow stronger. Growth will come easier and more quickly if you live in truth.

"Don't expect from people what they don't have to give. They do not hold your self-esteem or your value. They can only encourage you to find yours, as I placed it within you.

"Unnecessary time and spirit are spent trying to change others, rather than letting them be who they are. The only person you can change is

yourself. Do not expect a teacher to be a baker nor the builder to grow fruit. That can create a losing situation and sets people up for failure.

"A good parent does not participate in creating weak and whiny children. Therefore, I will not help you to be fragile. I will cheer you on and beam with pride when you are courageous.

"Life is the journey of finding the answers yourself. Sometimes you acquire them through trial and error, and many times, your discovery happens easily. The answers reveal themselves when you are ready.

"A good parent gives you the tools to become the best you can be. I gave you all the tools you need to become wise and compassionate. I gave you life, a body and free will. You have the tools. Why do you ask Me to use them for you?

"Most of you live in gratitude for the abundance of your life. I am so proud of you, my children. Keep growing, sharing and supporting each other.

"Eradicate negative energy by bombarding it with constructive, meaningful power. Do not ignore it. Point out the positive. Encourage it to step into the forefront. In that way, the Light will be greater than the dark.

"Just ask, and the answer will be revealed in its own time, the time that is in the highest good. Then, I will step back to allow you the free will to do as you choose.

"When you talk to Me or ask for help, I will always listen. I know what is in your heart and soul. Perhaps it would be wise for you to pray and listen. Only then can you truly hear me. How can I answer if you are not listening? When you cannot feel Me or hear Me, it is because you have turned up the noise from external sources or fear held in your mind, not your soul.

"You asked for the opportunity to learn compassion, and yet you ask Me why there are hungry children in the world. This is your opportunity to share what you have in abundance.

"Those of you who have an illness or disabilities are in a position to learn advanced lessons. People that surround you will also have the opportunity to add to their wisdom. Would you have Me take this away?

"Some ask for help to be strong and healthy. I gave you a mouth and the ability to open or close it and hands that have free will to pick up food or leave it on the table. The beauty of the outdoors is to encourage you to walk, play and exercise your body. I give you clean fresh air to breathe and wholesome food to nourish you. What else would you have Me do?

"Many ask for more money to buy more things, a bigger house, a new car, and vacations in faraway places. Many of those things damage the Earth. You pray to Me for a solution to make it right again. I have given you the tools and power to fix all that is broken.

"I will comfort you in times of need. I encourage you to move forward strong and whole, without fear. There is no room for fear between us. I love you always and without fail."

To illustrate how God's help can appear in your life, I would like to share a simple story, told many times on the Earth Campus, that demonstrates the partnership between the Light and souls when they request God's help.

Once, a great flood swept through a small town in Maryland. A man sought refuge on his rooftop to avoid being carried away by the swift current. He prayed to God to save him, but the water kept rising. In the distance, he saw a small boat heading in his direction. As it drew near, the man in the boat called to him, "Do you need help?" The man replied, "No, I am fine. I prayed to God, and I have complete faith He will save me." The man in the boat shook his head and left.

As the minutes ticked by, the floodwaters continued to rise, until the roof was half covered by water. A rescue helicopter spotted the man and dropped a rope for him to grab, so he could be lifted to safety. Again, the man said, "No thank you, I have faith that God will save me. Go and help someone else."

The water finally reached the last square of roof. The man was swept downstream and perished. When he found himself face-to-face with God, he asked Him, "Why did you not save me? I never lost faith that You would help me?"

God replied, "I sent you a boat and a helicopter."

I encourage you to keep moving forward in a positive frame of mind and soul. Do not lose focus because of worry, fear, or financial strain. Stay in the energy of love and gratitude, regardless of your outer circumstances, and your soul journey will be enhanced.

Higher Self

The Soul is Whole

Growing and Flourishing

We are each an individual soul, amidst a structured community, a society of souls that interact. The whole of your soul is your "Higher Self," the complete you that is aware of all you have witnessed since the moment of your creation. Your Higher Self is composed of the Creator's energy, and the energy you have gathered, in the whole of your existence added to it. Your soul remembers all your experiences—none are lost.

Your Higher Self has many parts to it; joy, guilt, courage, fear, fortitude, love and balance are but a few. You did not send your entire Being to Earth School. Depending on what subjects your Higher Self decided you would work on during this lifetime, you chose the appropriate parts of your Being to send for education. These elements were then separated from the whole of your Being and became your astral soul. Your astral soul is a part or parts of the Higher Self that separate for the purpose of attending Earth School.

You sent your astral soul to School to a human body to experience new ways of Being which could result in growth for your soul.

Why then not send the whole of your Being? Here are a few reasons:

- If you remembered and were conscious of everything you had witnessed and known, from the moment you came into Being, your experience in School would not be the same. Studying a limited number of subjects is more manageable and makes your experience more profound.

- When life begins from a seemingly blank slate or what seems to be the beginning, your focus is more on what can be, rather than what was.

- That separation of Higher Self and astral soul allows you to focus on the tasks at hand, which are the classes you chose to study. We tend to try harder when we do not have all the answers.

- When we are comfortable, we tend to become complacent and do not expand our horizons as much to discover what we have the potential to become.

- Not knowing can stir your curiosity and encourage you forward to better define yourself.

- If your astral soul encounters a shattering occurrence on Earth, your Higher Self is protected on the soul dimension.

Let's compare the flow of energy on Earth and how it relates to the flow of energy from your Higher Self.

On the Earth Campus, some energy is generated at a power plant by moving energy—pumping water through turbines that create electrical power. That energy is then split and flows to several power stations. There, it divides and travels to substations. Once more, it splits and moves from transformers to fuse boxes in thousands of houses and buildings. Then, it divides to send power to many outlets and switches in those structures. It is all the same energy from the same source, used for many purposes and is in more than one place at the same time.

You decide how you use the energy that streams to your house. Turn on the light, plug in the toaster, watch television, keep the food cold in your refrigerator or bake a cake in your oven. If you spread that power in too many directions, your fuse box overloads, and your house will have no power. You have to turn off some of the electrical units you had running, fix the breaker and try again.

Just like the power plant, the energy of your Higher Self divides and flows to the many aspects of you. Your flow of energy, your Higher Self, also came from one place, the Creator. The act of creation caused energy to move and expand, and it continues to flow from that source.

Much like the fuse box, the energy held in your body is limited. You choose how you use it. If you expend energy in too many directions, you risk becoming overloaded. Most people have a hard time simultaneously balancing their energy in different ways. They can be physically driving their car, mentally thinking about paying the bills, emotionally content, and spiritually looking for their purpose—all at the same time. Staying in the moment and not scattering your energy in this manner is more comfortable and less confusing. Taking the time to practice being in the present moment is well worth it.

In addition, be careful of people, places, circumstances or things that drain your energy. You may risk feeling depleted and not have the energy or presence to live your life.

Consider how Students attend college. They do not take all of their classes in one semester. Taking 500 units of study all at once is impossible and confusing. Students would be overloaded and unable to perform adequately. Rather, they make the experience manageable by spreading classes out over a period of years and limiting what they encounter.

Those of you, who gave thought and care to plan your Soul Classes, may have realized your best option was to start at the beginning and learn a few steps at a time. That way, you were less likely to become overwhelmed or discouraged.

Once you are on Campus, if you make the effort to address each of your subjects, you have the potential to become healthy, vibrant and glowing with wisdom. When you are in the human body, most of you can strengthen your muscles with exercise, your mind with study and your emotions with love. However, some individuals end up with a strong body, a weak mind, and a fragile emotional state. The knowledge you gain is then integrated into the whole of your soul in the afterlife and changes the illumination of your soul.

Depending on your course of study, your spirit can end up containing both the brightness of great compassion and the shadows of little tolerance, the capacity for immense love and the absence of confidence. Try to find balance in all areas as you move forward.

Remember, the real reason you are in Earth School—for your soul to experience, learn and create. Symbolically, you gather threads of experience, piece by piece, and your Higher Self weaves those threads together to create the tapestry that represents your wholeness. In other words, while you are consciously involved in the detailed work of growing, your Higher Self addresses the bigger picture of your existence.

When I was a little girl, I rode with my Dad to the corner gas station every Saturday morning. Back then, attendants would greet you, fill up your tank, check the oil and clean your windshield.

The employee who usually serviced our car was around sixty years old. That was the only job he ever had. After work, he would grab a hamburger at the corner stand, drive home, pet the dog, and head for his recliner to watch television for the remainder of the evening. After the 11 o'clock news, he went to bed. Perfectly content, he maintained his routine for thirty years, five days a week. As time went on, I formed an opinion about that man. I remember thinking what a shame it was that he was wasting his life. I did not know that his soul was fully illuminated, except for one subject, "To Be Content (with what is)." He was doing exactly what he came to do.

Each soul attends Earth School for a unique reason. Remember that if you decide to judge someone.

Earth is three-dimensional. That is one of the reasons you have a three-dimensional body. It holds your astral soul energy as you move around in School.

Where is your Higher Self right now? Some of you are from a higher vibration of spirit, referred to as a higher level of Light. If that plane is where your soul dwells, you have added Light, wisdom, knowledge and positive energy to your soul through your experiences and choices. There are many levels of higher Light. They can be compared to being in kindergarten, first grade, all the way up to graduate school. Upon creation, you began your soul journey just above the dividing line between Light and dark. The energy you create determines where your Higher Self resides on the realms of Light or shadow.

Compare these levels to neighborhoods on Earth. Some areas are geared towards family and raising children, while others can be infested with crime, violence or pollution. A variety of neighborhoods exist for the elderly, financially wealthy, the middle class and those who struggle to maintain a roof over their heads. Usually financial ability determines where you live.

On the energetic planes, where the spirit lives on without a body, neighborhoods are referred to as *levels* of Light or dark. Here, rather than money, illumination or the lack, thereof, determines which dimension of Light or dark you have attained.

Is your Being 20% illuminated, 30% shadowed, 40% light and 10% dark? Every combination is possible. Your past encounters and decisions make the difference. Did your words, thoughts and actions dim or brighten the environment?

If you have a lower vibration of spirit, your Higher Self would settle into a lower level. The lower your spirit vibrates, or the more negative energy you add to your soul, the further away from the Light you travel. Your Higher Self would then belong on a darker level.

Numerous planes of Light and dark exist beyond pure good and pure evil. Think of a dimmer switch on a chandelier. You have the choice to increase the energy from low light to the brightest light. But if you move from shadow to darkness, the reverse vibration goes from light gray to pure black.

Various planes of shadow and darkness hold the air of uncertainty, the fear of the unknown, or the hostility of prejudice. The dark planes can contain some negativity or be gorged with it. The Light levels contain the knowing of peace or are populated by Beings of integrity and grace. Will you stand in the company of thieves or scholars? Will your energy create a violent landscape or a soft haven? Will you live in erratic instability or richness of purpose? Will you create disquiet in your environment by choosing chaotic energy? Mixed energy creates uncertainty and anxiety, since its flow has no clear objective.

Most likely, you chose to take this trip to Earth School to learn more at a faster rate so you can attain the level of light or dark you wish to achieve.

With positive intentions and thoughts, kind and loving words and compassionate actions, you create and add more illumination and wisdom to your Being. This activity elevates your position on the levels of Light. Imagine how powerful and strong your Being can become with the opportunities available to you. Envision bringing all of that back to your Higher Self and to the Creator to add to the Light and flow of the Universe.

Imagine all the souls that can build on what you have to share. We are all connected. The Universe expands with our energy. What I fail in, depletes you. What you gain, strengthens me. That dynamics is the compilation of the Unity of Souls. We need to help and support each other for the highest good of all Beings.

This is the story of a woman who became an example to many people:

Grace considered herself a fortunate woman. She lived in a modest home perched upon a hilltop. Two rocking chairs, one for company and one for her, sat on her front porch. She routinely spent time each day, sitting in her chair with a homemade cookie and glass of iced tea. The view that stretched before her calmed her spirit. Life was good.

Every Tuesday, she made her way to town to purchase her weekly supplies. Once, she decided to drive by the local nursery to look at the flowers. In a wooden barrel by the cash register, she saw bags of tulip bulbs—10 for $1.00. She thought tulips would look pretty growing in *front of her porch and bought five bags.*

That Saturday, she got her hand spade and garden gloves from her tool shed and began planting the bulbs. Grace dug one hole at a time, dropped in a bulb, and patted the dirt back over it. After thirty holes, her back began to tire, but she was determined to finish. A few hours later, all the tulip bulbs were in the ground. In the weeks that went by, she pulled a few weeds that might interfere with the growth of the flowers and made sure to give them water.

Soon enough, green sprouts, seeking sunlight, were poking up through the dirt. That spring, she had a tulip patch in the front of her house—forty-two vibrant tulips and eight bulbs that failed to grow.

Each year, she added new bulbs and her garden grew. She planted each one herself, one at a time. Grace tended to her flowers every day. Most thrived, but every year, a few failed to bloom.

Twenty years passed. Now, on any given spring day, you will find people lined up on the road to gaze in awe at the hillside covered in thousands of tulips. They usually ask Grace the same question. How could one person accomplish such an enormous amount of work? She replies, "Just one at a time, a little at a time, and soon it created great beauty on a once plain rise."

That splendor also attracted the attention of the surrounding communities, and they sought her advice on how to complete such an incredible feat. Her persistence has encouraged more people to create beauty like she did, in their own way.

...And so it is with your Higher Self. If you work a little at a time and continue to pursue your goals, in the end you will have a stunning accumulation of accomplishments. Be present in this moment, just this one, and the moments will add up until you are filled with the beauty of your journey. Methodically weed out what you do not aspire to be.

You can become what you wish to be

One thought at a time

One intent at a time

One act at a time

Aspire to become enlightened

One Class at a time

One lesson at a time

One journey at a time

Better yourself one action at a time

One moment at a time

One hour at a time

One day at a time

...And the days will add up. Your thoughts will take root and grow. Your intentions will come to fruition, and your moments will be profound and filled with purpose. All of that will be added to your Higher Self.

The Human Body

A magnificent gift to treasure,

as your soul is held within

When we arrive at Earth School, we receive the primary gifts of life, and a human body in which our soul resides. We need a physical body to attend Earth School not only to hold our soul, but also to provide us with complex Classes such as Balance, Focus and the aspects of Love.

Your body is a house in which you live. However, you are not the house, and if the house were destroyed, you would still exist and move on.

You want to keep your body as healthy and balanced as possible. But know that it is only a tool for you to use and not your true self. Your soul is your actual self. If you lost an arm, would you still be you? What would happen if you lost a kidney, a leg or a breast? If you had a heart transplant, who would you be? Even your brain is a part of your mortal body that will expire as all physical matter dissipates. Your entire human form is substance that will wither and cease to exist. All the exterior parts are expendable. Which part would have to be removed for you to no longer be you? The answer is your soul.

However, your physical form can still be viewed as the vehicle for your soul and as such, needs daily attention and maintenance. It can get you from place to place. It allows you to balance the partnership between the body and soul, which provides you with Classes to learn on many levels—physically, emotionally, mentally and spiritually. Take good care of your physical form. You only get one on this journey.

We can see or touch our physical body, but we cannot see its emotional, mental and spiritual aspects. Earth Students who become obsessed with their appearance, can become overly attached to their exterior image. They can become judgmental or become distracted by visible difference between Students. It is not uncommon for them to spend considerable energy and money attempting to enhance their physical appearance. If they applied the same energy to their souls, the results could be amazing. Remember that beauty goes much deeper than our skin. It begins from and with the soul.

The emotional feature of your body is the part that experiences feelings. This aspect of self might cause tears to flow when you are sad or to radiate joy by smiling when you are happy. Earth School provides a full spectrum of Classes in emotion—from irritation to compassion, fear to contentment, and love to loss. You emotions will reveal themselves in your physical expressions, in the way you stand, the tone of your voice, the look on your face, your posture and the tilt of your head.

Your physical structure also houses its mental element. This part will experience lessons that can help you decide which way to go, how much money to spend, how to manage your time and much more. Your brain chemistry, flow, function, and health affect that part of you. Which part of the brain is dominant in you, the artistic right side or the logical left side? As the human form evolves, using both sides equally is not unusual. Right now, Students only use a small portion of their brain capacity. Yet, many people struggle to balance that fraction.

The lessons to be learned in racing thoughts, fear, worrying, calculating and anticipating are difficult, but well worth the work to become knowledgeable in those areas.

Mental checks and balances are important for maintaining a healthy existence. Consider occasionally turning off the outside chatter of media, cell phones and commotion, to allow your soul to be felt and heard.

There are many challenging tests to take while you are in physical form. When you are in the body, you might feel that you are your mind and your thoughts. However, your brain is only part of your physical form, like your hands. When you do not need your hands, you lay them down or let them hang at your sides. If you do not need your mind to actively process information, let it be silent.

Your brain's job is to control your body function, not your soul. If you ask another person to "point to yourself," the individual invariably aims a finger at the upper part of the abdomen. That is the area of their physique in which the soul resides. Very few would point to the brain. Most students are aware, at least on a subconscious level, that they are not their brain, but rather a soul held in their solar plexus area.

One day, you will graduate from Earth School, and your mortal body will cease to function. Your brain will also die. However, your soul will hold what you have learned and continue. For that reason, consider giving your time and energy to your soul's growth. The faster you learn to calm your mind, the more you will be in tune with your soul and your purpose for Being.

Imagine giving all your energy to your brain and thoughts while you are in School, only to learn that when you graduate all that is left behind.

Now, imagine giving all your time and energy to your soul. When you graduate, you take everything.

The spiritual aspect of your body shows in the way you live your life. How does your living show gratitude for the chance to attend Earth School? Do you nurture your body with good nutrition and surround yourself with positive people? Do you keep your environment clean and free of clutter? Do you live your life consciously, acknowledging that your human form is a temporary gift meant to help you accomplish spiritual lessons and enlightenment? Do you embrace this opportunity to learn? Spiritual courses come in every shape and form.

I urge you to use your mind to think,

your emotions to feel,

and your soul to know.

Many people place the greatest burden on the body's mental aspect. Most of us encounter episodes when our minds chatter constantly. Problems arise when the mind steps to the forefront, out of fear, in the attempt to control our journey. The optimal way to achieve harmony between the physical, emotional, mental and spiritual aspects of the human body is to live from your soul. This course continues throughout your lifetime giving you many opportunities to become wiser.

Let's discuss how this works in Earth School. If your physical body develops a virus, it deals with the symptoms-

runny nose, cough, aches and pains. Your mental feature can decide what medication to take or how much rest is needed to heal. The spiritual portion can focus on the opportunity for healing. The emotional aspect can stay calm, knowing this will pass. Your soul can be in the moment observing, learning and participating in yet another lesson to experience.

However, achieving harmony between the physical, mental, emotional and spiritual functions is not always that easy. If one part goes into fear, the other aspects start to react. For example, the more difficult way to get through a virus would be for the physical body to have the symptoms. Your mental facet can then fret over the cold turning into pneumonia. Your emotional side might go into fear worrying about potential side effects. Your spiritual aspect might wonder why God put you in a situation that feels bad and how unfair life is.

Having all your aspects in alignment and present in the moment feels most comfortable and indicates that you have learned to practice balance. You are present in that moment to read your book—physically, emotionally, mentally, and spiritually. If instead you are physically reading a book, mentally thinking about the chores yet to be done, emotionally upset at a friend, and spiritually feeling empty—you are scattered.

The human form can offer its own challenges. There is a delicate balance between physical wants versus the true needs of the body and the soul. Physical wants can lead to a wide variety of cravings; including food, drink, people, shopping, power, possessions, sex and drugs. Do you choose your highest good or immediate gratification? Resolving to live your best life is a Class well learned.

Your body also serves as a hazard light for your soul. Headaches, neck pain and illness are often the symptoms that appear to draw attention to a real, underlying problem. They may indicate you are on a path that is not in your highest good or moving into an unhealthy situation. Stress in the form of these symptoms can be a sign to slow down, breathe and look at the larger picture.

That is not to say that the human form does not have inherent physical problems. It does. Genetics and the environment play a role in that. Your body will present lessons to you in many forms. Learn everything you can.

The human body multi-tasks, provokes thought, seeks pleasure, drives emotion, activates sensation and informs you. How you decide to use this instrument is your choice.

Those of you in the accelerated program in Earth School might have noticed that some part of your body may not work as you think it should. Consider another way of perceiving the situation. Perhaps what you see as defective gives you the extra edge to learn more complicated lessons than Students who do not have an obstacle to overcome.

The many parts of your body are the outward expressions of your soul. The joy, stress, peace or turmoil inside of you will be evident in and on your body. The outside is influenced by your essence, your soul. Inner beauty and peace emanate from the soul. They will show on your face and in the way you move, speak, touch and love.

Many of you were born into a family with a mother and father. Some of you have siblings. A few of you chose to begin Earth School without a family unit already in place. As time goes on, you might find that your family dynamic was meant to be that way to provide you with special circumstances in which to learn.

Our families come as many types—biological, chosen, neighbors, friends or any group or pairing that comes together to love and support. I hope wherever you were born, you were loved, welcomed and treasured.

In the not so distant past, many parents commonly looked at their new baby as a blank slate. They believed they had a responsibility to form the child with beliefs that society dictated, or their idea of what their child should be.

As a result, many people were not raised in a nurturing environment that supported who they truly are and were meant to be. Some choose to stay stuck in bitterness because of this lack of early support, and some choose to learn from it. Both are a choice. More than a few of those children grew into grown-ups who spent much of their adult life trying to heal the wounds of childhood. Countless souls graduate from the Earth Campus, without ever having lived their truth and feel lost and disconnected from their true self, their soul. This is a difficult way to live.

Today, in many instances, the attitude about how best to raise children has shifted. Now, many parents are interested in their child's talents, innate abilities, interests and passions.

If this more supportive approach was not your experience, you can always go on the amazing journey to discover yourself. Learning who you are, as well as what you do and do not want in your life, can be transforming.

A few of you chose Classes that include being born with your own sense of self and follow that through your life without deferring to your environment. Think how far you might go if you do not get distracted, if you stay the course and keep moving forward.

Remember, however you use it, your physical form is a gift for a limited time, so use it wisely. Your mortal body may get worn out, but your wisdom of soul can get stronger and wiser. After all, that is the point of Earth School. Appreciate what is yours while you have it.

Foundations

Support your soul and body well

An oak tree lives on St. Johns Island near Charleston, South Carolina. Over 1400 years old, it is known as the Angel Oak and stands as a beautiful example of a strong foundation and healthy energy flow.

The tree grew from the energy of a single acorn buried in the ground. It began by putting down a root system, then rose up from the dirt, reaching to be more, splitting in many directions and growing more vibrant. This helped to anchor and develop a strong base for the tree.

Its roots grew sturdy, fibrous and entrenched in the soil to absorb nutrients and water. Without this strong foothold, the tree would have been weak and small. You cannot see the root system, because it is hidden beneath the ground. What is visible is what sprang from the foundation—the trunk, bark, branches and leaves. Altogether, they offer cover and beauty and reflect the change of seasons.

With each passing year, the tree took the opportunities its environment offered. It used the condition of the sun, soil and rain to strengthen and fortify itself. As the seasons slipped by, some of the limbs became so large and heavy that the tree was in jeopardy of splitting apart. Instead, the limbs turned and curved downward until they braced themselves on solid ground. Then, they turned once more and continued their upward growth. This gave the tree added balance and strength.

The tree has supported itself so well that it cannot fall over. Wind that could have blown it over when it was young, now only rustles it leaves. It stored up energy not needed in the moment to feed it in harsh conditions and it thrived in mild ones.

The Angel Oak has survived floods, hurricanes, earthquakes, swarms of insects, disease and human intrusion. All the parts work in unison to create a powerful, viable presence. It exudes the energy of strength, longevity and harmony, and it all sprouted from the potential inside of one acorn.

And so it is with you. Your soul might seem small right now, but you sprout from your Higher Self, the whole of your soul. When you are on the Earth Campus, you grow and create the energy flow of your journey from your intentions and actions. You do this by attending Classes and paying attention to lessons presented to you as a Student of Earth School. Gaining wisdom from those lessons helps you define your foundation so that you can evolve to be as strong a presence as the Angel Oak. Use the opportunities presented to you to learn, understand and become wiser. Keep all of your parts in balance and harmony. Thrive and be healthy in all of your aspects.

Strive for a true sense of self, not one that has been put upon you by any another person, environment or distraction. Live your true life, with your own knowing, and sense of self. Many Students are living a life based on outside energy, and the expectations and beliefs of others.

When that happens, you are not living your truth, but merely existing in the energy of other Students. How many people spent the first part of their lives doing what they were told, only to run into a mid-life crisis trying to determine who they really are?

Instead, imagine support from the day you were born to follow your soul, encouragement to think for yourself and kindness to support your School journey. It is so easy to slip into something that is set for us, rather than to follow our own course. Often, we have to break apart that old foundation and start from the ground up, carefully selecting a base of self-truth. Otherwise, we risk building our foundation on something that is distorted or foreign and not true and wise.

Will you shape your foundation on ground that is solid, strong and unshakable, or on sand that easily shifts and changes? Is one better than the other? Anything and everything can change in School in an instant. If that happens, will your base support you?

Consider this: Many Students put their energy into the part you see—their physical body, the style of their hair, the car they drive, and the house they live in. They ignore the part they cannot see—their soul and its growth.

If you asked them who they were, where they came from and where they are going, chances are, countless Students would not know. They base their worth and success on the material, on visible things that do not last, including financial wealth. They have yet to discover they are experiencing lessons for the benefit of their Being, their attainment of Light. Life can bombard you with the distractions of the material world. They are what is immediately in front of you.

Commonly, you develop your foundation based on what you are told as a child. Society influences most of us concerning how and where to live, whom to shun or whom to relate to. Culture, religion, low self-esteem, giving your energy away, copying your parent's foundation and society's standards can find their way into your groundwork.

Children believe what they are told. "You are beautiful." "You are stupid." "You are loved." "You were a mistake." "You have a gentle heart." Think before you label people. Point out the positive, and they will most likely follow that energy. Point out the negative, and they will believe you and begin to shape their foundation based on what they see and hear.

Some Students have formed inner voices that tell them they are unattractive or have no value. This can be a Class on discovering distractions, the power to overcome negativity and the strength to conquer that which is damaging. What they feel on the inside has been reinforced from the outside. Help others to recognize the good in themselves. If we all follow our positive aspects, imagine what the world could be.

A grammar school teacher asked her students to write their name on the top of a piece of paper and pass it to the student on their right. Each pupil was to write something they admired about that person, and so it continued around the classroom. Then, the paper was given back to the child.

Twenty years later, the teacher ran into one of the students from that class. He pulled his wallet out and showed her the worn paper the students had written on that day. He had not known someone thought he was smart and funny or that people liked and valued him as a person, until he read that paper. It had become one of his most prized possessions. It changed his perspective and in turn, changed his life. It fortified his foundation with positive, truthful energy.

Here are a few questions to contemplate:

- What will be your foundation?

- Do you have a clear view of who you are?

- Where did you come from and what are you hoping to accomplish in Earth School?

Without answers to those questions, you might form your life on weak, crumbling, unbalanced, flawed or undefined energy.

As you become your true self, contemplate building your foundation not on what you were told, but on what you choose is right for you in this moment. If your old base has cracked and deteriorated over the years, form a new one with all the knowledge and insight you have gathered. Some Students are happy to stand on the same groundwork they built as a child throughout their lives. You always have options. Here are examples of different types of foundations that are important for a well-rounded education on the Earth Campus:

Your physical stability begins with your body. Your body's corporeal strength depends on its core, which supports the body's whole. The body's core serves as the foundation for your extremities. If that base becomes weak, the rest of the body is affected. Muscles, which support the frame of your physique, should be kept as robust as possible. A powerful base helps to keep your physical form healthy and energized.

Another type of physical foundation is the house or building where you live.

Let me tell you about The House of Everything. Adam was forty years old when he found his dream beach house—and it was for sale. It is what he had always desired, and now, he thought he would be truly happy.

All the rooms were measured and paint samples were gathered. Shopping for furniture, light fixtures and windows, while envisioning where they would be displayed, gave him great joy. However, Adam did not check the home's foundation or the condition of the structure. All he could imagine was how proud he would be of his House of Everything when it was done. Everyone would admire it and be impressed with his accomplishment.

Adam calls it his House of Everything because that is what it took—everything—all of his time, hopes, dreams, passion, energy and money. Adam spent his days working to pay for the house and nights renovating it.

His life revolved around his house, and he had little time or energy for anything else. Adam lost focus on his journey. For some reason, he thought he would feel settled when his dream became reality.

Shells and starfish were collected to decorate the windowsills, but Adam did not notice the wood was rotted. Crown molding was added to the rooms, however, he did not know that the walls were full of termites. Adam did not consider what he could not see. He focused on the surface, but ignored the foundation that was supposed to support everything.

One winter night, a severe storm came ashore where Adam's House of Everything stood and eroded the weak structure, one wave at a time. The dwelling crumbled into the water and washed away. When the house and all that Adam owned was gone, he felt empty. He had not balanced his life.

What he discovered was that these were lessons he had come to Earth School to walk through. He needed to learn to be whole, healthy and happy regardless of what was outside of him. Every abode, person and circumstance will come and go, and his value was not dependent on them. Adam had defined himself by the structure in which he lived, but it was just wood and nails, nothing of true value. His response to outside illusions kept him distracted. The devastation of his material world helped him to refocus on what was truly valuable—the education and journey of his soul. That night was another gift of a lesson to be learned.

Physical foundations can be seen and touched. However,

as the House of Everything story reveals, many of life's supports lie in the unseen.

Here is my best advice regarding emotional foundations. Relationships are a big part of Student life. Whether they are with a parent, friend, partner or foe, this aspect of your base will most likely be important to you. However, do not look to others to complete you, because when they leave, the place you allowed them to fill in you will be vacant.

A person without a strong emotional foundation or root system, can base their self-esteem on how they perceive others view them. Are they physically attractive? If they do not meet society's norms, they might feel something is wrong with them. Soon, their perception of their true value plummets. If they feel unaccepted in the traditional sense—material assets, family, social standing and job expectations, they might feel as if they are a failure. They can now easily be blown over by life's challenges. Their view of life becomes convoluted when they adhere to the standards society has set, rather than to those of their Being.

If you nurture and strengthen your support, recognizing this journey is your opportunity to become strong and wise, then you will be like the Angel Oak. You will stand on your own, ever reaching out and up, without fear, knowing that the base you grew from is solid and will support you in tough conditions.

The truth is everyone in your life will come and go. They might leave Earth School before you or move across the Earth Campus. You might come home first, or leave to start a new adventure. An argument might end a friendship.

People will walk into your life and depart as they continue their own journey. On the Earth Campus, you are the only person you will always have. Given this truth, consider giving yourself everything you need to be whole, healthy and happy. That way, people coming and going in your life will not damage your emotional footing. If you depend on another person to make you feel strong, stable or loved, what will you do when one of you moves on? Instead, view what they offer you as icing on the cake, an extra boost, and companionship for that time.

What a healthy and positive relationship might provide for you is another soul to walk along side of you for a period. This person can encourage and strengthen you for the present and future, inspire you to be the best you can be, and when seeing your potential, encourage you further than you thought possible. Other people can mirror what you cannot see for yourself and love who you are. Relationships in all its forms is a tremendous gift. Be grateful for those you have now, knowing tomorrow might be different.

Even more important to building a strong emotional foundation is discovering and acknowledging your own value and uniqueness. Realize that you already have everything you need to move forward. Don't look to other people to gauge your worth, as you hold it inside of you. You do not need to accept relationships that are toxic or damaging just to have someone in your life.

Many Students on the Earth Campus struggle with self-esteem—which is actually their course for defining their true self. Some settle for damaging associations with other people to avoid being alone. However, being with yourself can be rewarding. When you are alone, cherish your time. Treat yourself with care and respect. This can be your moment to create balance and clarity, to examine your priorities, to practice peace and to nurture the whole of yourself.

In addition to your physical and emotional supports, your mental foundation needs attention. Do you allow your mind to chatter constantly, or do you use it as it was meant to be used—to process information and resolve problems? Do you overload your mind and risk damaging the whole of you? Do you focus on fear instead of reality? Inner balance helps you keep your intellectual processes healthy.

Fear is one of the greatest threats to good mental health. It can keep you stuck in an unhealthy place or relationship. Focus your thinking on the reality of a situation and not on the energy of anxiety. Ninety percent of everything you dread will never happen. That is a lot of time and energy wasted.

If you stand in your kitchen preparing lunch and your mind worries about something that is not happening, your thought is faulty. You have no basis for it, other than the fear that it could happen. You do not need to be the conduit for nuisance energy that is not part of your present moment. Paying attention to a conduit of Universal energy can bring it towards you.

Like energy attracts like energy. Universal energy is the compilation of all resources that exist. That includes positive and negative dynamics. When your thoughts dwell on and bring forth Universal energy that is harmful, take control, or you will empower it to become part of you, thereby giving it your strength. Strongly say, "These are not my intended thoughts; this is not my intended goal." Until your mind is quiet and your soul is creating your life.

Another critical base that requires your care and consideration is your spiritual foundation. Some people look to other students for support in finding and strengthening their connection to the Creator, and many recognize their own personal relationship with The Light. A considerable number have devoted their lifetimes to searching for divine substance that answers their questions about the meaning of life and sustains them on their life journey. Other students have opted to go it alone, without spiritual awareness. Whatever you choose, remember how loved you are.

When creating all aspects of your life's foundation, don't forget that you can stand on the shoulders of those who have gone before you. You can learn and be lifted by those who impart their wisdom to you. In addition, remember that you, too, can provide the shoulders of wisdom and support for those who come after you. Stand proud on your foundation, and reach as high as you can.

Energy

Create with your Life

Everything in the Universe is composed of energy. That is a fact. It can be whole galaxies or a single blade of grass, the planet Earth or a drop of water. The human body, the intensity of a voice, your presence—all of it is composed of energy in its many forms

Your soul energy came from the pure Light of the Creator. Hence, your soul is Creator energy. That Light force gives you the power to create, and your life provides the opportunity. The question is—how will you choose to use your creative power? The Universe is ever changing through you, with you and because of you. It continues and expands, and that flow, in itself, is the act of creation.

The purpose of Earth School is to create new energy with your life. Each day in Earth School is an opportunity to decide who you will be by the actions you take, the thoughts you think and the words you chose to speak. If you do not mindfully choose what you design, you run the risk of creating random and chaotic energy.

How will you choose to divide and spend your day? Here is one possibility: 25% working, 10% with family, 4% in quiet stillness, 7% worried, 5% eating, 10% joyful, 25% sleeping, 3% angry, and 11% learning.

You decide how to manage your time and energy—mind, body, and spirit. Then focus your vitality in the direction you have chosen. Be aware of each moment, so your day does not slip away unnoticed. We hear many Earth Students wondering where their time went. One day your children are small, and before you know it, they have little ones of their own. Life happens, whether you manage it or not.

Consider living a life with direction and purpose, while you are fully present. Be the conscious creator of your journey. Have a determination that no matter what happens, you will move forward through your day in the best possible way. Be strong, clear, and grateful for this opportunity to be attending Earth School.

In your everyday life, contemplate leaving space for new energy to come in.

- Clear your mind to create room for your soul to be heard.

- Clear your body of toxins so health can thrive.

- Clear your emotions of fear so you are present in each moment.

- Clear your house of clutter to make space for new vitality to enter your life.

- Clear your life of negativity to make room for positive energy.

If all of your places, inside and out, are packed full, where will you have space for the new? How will you be able to process new information? If you hang onto things, thoughts, emotions or spiritual fears from the past, you will not have room for the present or future. The past may be your comfort zone, but it can feel emotionally devastating for some people. You might even feel stuck. Ask for help and refocus on your present intention. Remember what you are experiencing is a lesson presenting you with new challenges.

Move forward. Even changing one thing at a time in your life is a start. Take baby steps if it helps. Make time and space for some silence and a quiet mind. Creative energy flows freely in stillness. In opening to the wealth of the Universe, anything is possible.

The Universe is designed to expand and become more. Scientists on Earth have now identified the edge of the Universe and are witnesses to its continuing expansion.

We are all Citizens of the Universe, meaning we are part of it. However, being a citizen comes with responsibility. On Earth, you may identify yourself as a citizen of a country, state, city or even community. Your citizenship associates you with where you reside. The people and places there will be affected by your presence and you by theirs. What you put into this place or take from it is up to you.

Earth School has much to teach us about interaction, connection, nurturing and beauty. However, the planet is dependent on the actions of its citizens. The Earth has many unhealthy areas right now because of the carelessness of some people. Students can help by changing their harmful actions and replacing them with positive interactions.

Remember, you are a conduit for energy. While you will not be able to control the power directed at you, what comes through you in response is your choice. What you create, what you participate in, and the words you speak are your choice.

Let's consider how energy moves. Creative energy comes from a void, a space yet to be filled. If you are not sure what to do with your creative power, just ask for guidance, wisdom or a new perspective.

If you generate positive, uplifting energy in your home, laughter will fill the air, happiness will settle onto your pillows, and peace and delight will surround you. When you fill your home with negative force through thoughts, actions or words, or you play movies, television or music that form rage, that energy will fill the air, settle onto your furniture, linger on your skin and swirl around your mind and soul. It is now part of your experience.

The drive of one person can make a difference even under seemingly insurmountable odds. In the recent past, a man aspired to be president of the United States. It was his hope and intent to help change the world. For political reasons, he was not given that office. His high aspirations ended abruptly.

Instead of walking away from public service, he refocused his energy and intentions and became active in creating a healthier Earth. When what he wanted to be was no longer an option, he moved forward with positive action. This has benefited the entire planet.

Sometimes in Earth School, what seems to be the worst event in your life might not be that at all. It may be your life force directing you to a higher calling and challenging you to grow. With hindsight, it can be miraculous.

You choose whether to take the high road, the low road, the middle road or switch back and forth. You decide on a slow, plodding, thoughtful pace or the fast track. Which is best for you? Physically, emotionally, spiritually and mentally, what is in your highest good?

Earth School Students tend to pass negative energy on quickly. Here is an example:

Your boss is rude to you in front of your co-workers. You hold that humiliation close to you for the rest of the afternoon. By the time you get into your car to drive home, you are seething. As you drive, another car forgets to signal, and your anger explodes. You honk your horn and shout rude words of your own.

When you get home, you are tired and want to relax, but the kids need your attention, and dinner is not making itself. The rest of the evening, the energy your boss directed at you hours before, now fills your house as you pass it on to your family ... and so it continues. Some Students allow that momentum to flow and color other parts of them, creating a series of thought forms.

Something like this, "My boss was rude. I hate my boss, my job, my work, and my life. I am miserable." Depression can set in and fill your world. This cycle all began because of a few negative words directed at you.

You allowed yourself to become the conduit for critical energy by passing it on. The more you participate in that process, the more critical force will find its way to you, knowing that you will pass it on, and it will expand. After all, that is how the Universe works. Just like water, energy flows to the path of least resistance, following and filling the course open to it. Creation is energy multiplying. The

Universe is expanding every second. It is the natural evolution of development.

Instead, you can take what is negative in your life and choose not to move it forward, you can end it and stop it cold. Refuse to be the conduit for it. As an alternative action, you can understand it is a lesson that has come to you for the sake of learning, for the growth of your Being. You might decide to form new, more positive energy, perhaps loving strength, and pass that on. Choose to be the conduit for love and more love will come to you, knowing that you will pass it on and it can expand as energy naturally does.

If you have a difficult time identifying energy, try this:

Imagine standing on the ground and looking up to the air above you. Picture a flexible conduit, the kind they use in construction to contain the wires running to outlets. The bottom of the conduit is above you. There are millions of tubes. Depending on where the conduit originates, the other end may go all the way up to the Highest Light, down to the darkest of realms or anywhere in-between. Each conduit has one type of power running through it. The energy cannot flow out of the conduit, unless you reach up and hold the bottom of it, allowing what force is in there to flow.

On the Earth Campus, many Students find themselves stuck in the memories of moments that took place years ago. They might dwell on a friends betrayal, seemingly unable to get rid of those thoughts. In that moment, you hold the conduit for past wounds. Let go of the conduit, and you will let go of the thoughts and energy.

Now, choose the kind of strength that will move you forward in the best possible way. Reach up and grab the conduits that you desire to engage. Perhaps you would like the power flowing from the conduit for clarity. All that outside energy needs is your permission to become part of you.

Whether the negative energy comes from food, family, job, an object or an experience, you can choose to filter out the negative effect. If you hang onto it or absorb it, you risk the harmful impact it can have on you, such as illness, lingering sorrow or other struggles. As an alternative, you can stop its flow, release its force, and replace it with positive vitality. Your choice makes the difference.

If your boss says or does something offensive to you, perhaps you could go for a walk before going home to re-focus and release the negative energy. That way, you do not move it forward. Remember, being around someone who is inappropriate can be a good test of staying in your own intended strength and character. Even better, maintain protection around your Being, so outside energy flows around you and not through you.

A large percentage of people that come to see me are carrying energy placed there by someone else. Here are a few common ones that I am shown:

- An energetic lock and chain around the throat area when a person has been stifled in speaking or expressing their true feelings.

- A damaged structure in the second chakra, about six inches above the tailbone when a person has been sexually mistreated.

- An arrow or knife in any area of the back when the person has lived in deception. This usually accompanies a sharp, physical pain.

- Facing backwards when they live in the past, not living in the present, but stuck in memories.

- Looking down and appearing dim when they are living with shame.

- Standing in mud up to their hips when they are stuck. This can present in physical, spiritual, emotional or mental exhaustion.

- A shadow looming over them when they are being victimized.

Greed, hate and envy are strong emotions that can turn into oppressive power commanding your full attention. On an energetic level, they have weight and can physically drain you, mentally agitate or be emotionally devastating. They exist to give us the opportunity to identify these energies, test your character, recognize your tools and decide how you will deal with negative events.

Resentment and anger can destroy you as much, or more, as the person you are directing them at. These emotions can stay inside you and eat away at you on many levels. I once heard a wise woman say, "Holding resentment is like taking poison and hoping the other person dies." Many of us experience these emotions. It is what you do with them that determine your character. Pay attention when they appear in your life. Experience their cause, determine what you will do when faced with these forces, and do the best you can to walk through them. If you are unsuccessful, gather experience and turn a negative into a positive. Determine to be what you choose and not someone who reacts without conscious intention.

Grief can be a crippling force that can permeate every part of your Being. When grief comes your way, try to accept it as part of your life experience. Use all the tools you have to walk through it. Ask for help from other Students and from all the Angels and souls in the Light. Learn all you can about grief, try to see it for what it truly is—a Class, a heartfelt, difficult course to walk through. Remember that, this feeling too, will change, and you will move forward into the next moments wiser or embittered.

Energy becomes part of you—the good and the bad, if you allow it. Once you absorb or allow negative power in or around you, how do you rid yourself of it? You will have to discover the best ways for you. You make the decision to keep it, act on it, react to it, pass it on or get rid of it. Students have come up with ingenious ways to clear themselves of energy they do not wish to carry forward.

Here are a few ways to visualize the movement of energy, that I have seen people use with success:

Mindfully throw negative energy away with intent.
Designate something, like a stop sign, you pass by daily,
and intend to leave your worries and negativity on the sign.
It will then stay outside of your home on that sign. When
you enter your house, you will keep peace and harmony
flowing there. The next time you see the stop sign, you can
pick up what you released on it, or decide you are done
with it and walk away. Your intent alone will make it so.

Use prayer flags. The Tibetan people handcraft silk prayer
flags as symbols of their intentions. After writing on the
silk, they hang the flag to be blown by the wind. Over the
seasons, the flag begins to fade and shred. By physically
creating the flag and every word on it, their intent is
solidified and visible. The power of the wind moves the
flag as a physical reminder of their goals. They believe the
vibration goes out into the world, creating the flow of the
written word.

Give yourself a shower of Light. Another way to clear
yourself is to intend that an energetic cascade of Light
washes away any foreign or negative energy that has stuck
to you.

Align yourself with the Creator. Stop and breathe.
Envision your soul Light in your lower chest. Sit in your
soul Light, focus with your soul, not from your mind. Let
your soul glow and beam straight up to the Highest Light.
In our everyday lives, many of us tend to send our focus,
beams of our soul Light, out to people, events and

problems—to what is here on this earthly plane. That scatters energy, takes attention from our soul journey and can overwhelm us.

What other people do with their lives can annoy you and take your focus. "They hurt my feelings." "They messed up my life." "They don't know what they are doing." When your soul is connected to the Highest Light, and only the Highest Light, we find ourselves, our purpose and the meaning of life. This connection is calm and clear.

Healing. The power of healing energy is being used more every day. Imagery and a positive attitude help you to heal faster on all levels. Your intent and strength flowing towards the goal of healing is part of the equation. Don't forget to use the powerful energy of gratitude as an opportunity to heal.

Joy, respect, and kindness are uplifting energies. They can generate a peaceful and nurturing environment in which you can heal and the soul can grow.

Breathe in what is healing and Light. Exhale what is old and negative.

Positive reminders. Having reminders in front of you of your aspirations and objectives can help to stay focused on your goal. Hanging a poster with a positive message, quotes from people you admire, or a picture that represents your goals will help you stay in healthy vitality.

Remember you are in Class. Do not get so caught up in life that you forget you are attending School to learn. Your lessons and courses are for your benefit, the betterment of your soul. All experiences and energy are meant to present you with the chance to become an enlightened Being.

Change your vibration. This is a good time to consider your personal energy vibration. It can be calm and steady, big and loud, scattered, or a combination. Each soul has its own unique vibration, which comes from your personal Being. Many souls gravitate to the same frequency, because it is where they feel comfortable.

You can easily change your soul vibration by taking an action that moves you to the flow you wish to have. Take a deep breath and slow your energy down. Pump up your energy by speeding up your breath. Then, mindfully move in the direction you choose. Breathing helps maintain the body, mind, and soul connection and builds balance.

Be in nature or in life's enjoyment. You can sit on the grass and breathe to calm and center yourself. Invigorate your Being by meeting with friends or taking a brisk walk. Hike in the mountains to reconnect to the Earth and release stress. Enjoy good food to feel your best. Laugh to enjoy your life and release endorphins for well-being.

Ask for help. Ask your Guardian Angel or those in the Light to assist you if you are feeling overwhelmed. Quiet your mind to just Be.

Flow with your own life energy. Do your best to flow with your life force, not the intensity of others or the environment that surrounds you. This will give you the true sense of being whole, healthy, happy and self-contained. Flowing in your own strength will keep you on your path and not swayed by outside influences.

Certain people try to match the drive of whatever person or place they are near. With each person, they are different, much like a chameleon. They become good at copying the force present in the moment, rather than remaining themselves. Students who live this way have not developed their sense of self and may not exert the effort to define themselves. Succumbing to peer pressure, mindless living or striving to fit in can be a waste of strength and spirit.

You can be swept up in another person's dominant energy. Some exude a robust presence, which can attract those with weaker energies. However, just because their presence is strong, does not mean it is good. Find your own powerful presence within you and remain yourself.

Some people become distracted in the power of the moment and end up doing things they had not intended. They are not confident to stand up and say, "No," when doing so would put them at odds with the status quo. Joining a group and following like cattle is easy. However, cattle mentality is mindless movement. Staying in your integrity and true self can be harder, but well worth the effort.

Fill yourself with your truth.

Send your children out into the world with a good sense of themselves, so they do not attach themselves to individuals who have stronger energy. Maintain regular communication with your children and help them to define their choices without peer pressure. Hold a safe space for them to find themselves. Give them love and support to define their ambitions in life. Encourage them to refine their gifts and soul Light

Ben came to see me when he was 42 years old. He had low energy and was uncertain of where to sit, where to rest his hands, to lean back or forward. Ben did not have a sense of himself. He wanted outside direction. His Angel told me that Ben was a timid soul, who found it easier just to do what he was told. That meant no decisions, no mistakes, uncomfortably moving through life. He had relied on other people to tell him what to think and how to act.

I was given permission to look at Ben's path in life. He was now at a fork in the road. On the current path, he wore a suit to work and sat in an office all day feeling no connection. On the other path, Ben wore a flannel shirt and jeans with hiking boots. Smiling and excited, he stood with a group of kids on the edge of a pond, teaching them about the plants that surrounded them.

One of Ben's gifts of Spirit was the ability to create splendor with colors, light, music, words—anything that is artistic in nature. Ben held a rare gift of beauty. This translated into Ben not only being here for his own soul growth, but also being on a mission to teach others about

the vitality of splendor. He knew that when you let beauty seep into your everyday life, it can enhance all that is.

When I relayed this to Ben, he began to cry. He said, "I always knew I was special, but didn't want to look foolish and tell people who I really am. I feel so alive in the outdoors and have wanted to teach botany and pass on information about the wondrous evolution of our planet. I took the office job because everyone told me to. I've wasted my life moving against what I knew to be true to please other people."

In truth, Ben had not wasted his life. He could use the past to strengthen his future resolve. That day, Ben received information on his source energy and left with a joyful determination to live his life in the way he chooses.

If you raise your children in love and respect, they will accept that as normal. If you raise your children with criticism and belittlement, that will be customary to them. They will look for that same energy when they go out in the world on their own. What would happen if you raised your children in mixed energy? Will that cause them to feel uncertain or chaotic? Be mindful of what you pass on as you raise the next generation.

Even too much of a good thing can present a challenge for a little one. Consider the excitement of a birthday, the biggest event in many children's lives. Balloons, relatives, cake, presents and attention from everyone surrounds them. The sensory load gets higher and louder, until the child feels bombarded by the energy and has a meltdown.

Anger and violent energy also scares children and stays with them for a long time. It changes who they are. Be gentle with babies and children. They respond positively to kindness and calm situations.

Over a lifetime, many Students experience the human need of wanting to be acknowledged and find both healthy and unhealthy ways to find acceptance. However, you only need to accept your true self, and the extraneous forces will fall away.

School is a time to face your strengths and weaknesses, your wisdom and ignorance. You will have a myriad of opportunities to test yourself in the Classes you attend.

If you are naturally angry, School is the opportunity to study all you can about the energy of anger. With new knowledge and understanding, you can change what you do not wish to be. When you know better, you tend to do better.

If you are inherently patient, Earth School is the perfect place to test yourself. If your neighbor calls you often to vent her needless frustration and to project it onto you, at what point will your patience run out? Should you continue to have patience? Sometimes, your most positive response means you need to stop being patient. End or limit toxic relationships to maintain your personal health, and direct your energy towards your life.

Your life force will challenge you to grow and survive. That life force is your soul vitality with a purpose. If you are aimless and feel unsettled, your life force will push you to find out what makes you feel complete. Feeling great passion is your life force telling you that you are on your path. There is more, go and find it.

What if you viewed your time in School as problem free, with many Classes and opportunities to challenge you? You would see your life for what it truly is—chances to acquire knowledge. Your attention would then be focused on the lesson at hand rather than the unfairness that seems to be in your life. Numerous Students fear they will be too weak to walk through some experiences, and they are afraid of the event itself. True strength is having the knowledge that no matter what happens, you will walk through it.

Many people in their mid-life find their life force rises to their conscious level to remind them to stretch and grow further than they have. Some refer to it as a mid-life crisis. I call it an awareness of purpose on a conscious level.

This awareness is an opportunity. Some embrace it and pursue more wisdom. Others use this time to try to recoup their youth. Whether you choose to be a wise elder or an old teenager is a choice. Souls at this stage might wonder aloud, "Is this all there is? Isn't there more?" Those questions can push them out of their comfort zone, hopefully to discover a new chapter in their life.

Energy can work in wonderful ways throughout our lives. Intending to create positive, loving energy around people, places and items has a lasting effect. Food or clothing made with love tastes and feels better. Even if you do not remember the hugs, love, kisses, and words directed at you as an infant, they stay in your energy and on your skin.

Children retain the dynamics of how situations felt. When your children make mistakes, they do not remember the problem, they remember how you made them feel about it. Did you criticize them or calmly teach them how to make better choices? Did you make it a learning opportunity or a chance to demean them?

Students in Earth School have begun to recognize the effect of energy in all areas of their lives. A current trend in the media is to produce television programming dedicated to teaching viewers how to create a clean, organized and clutter-free home. After clearing and cleansing, the space is redecorated with color and just enough items to enhance the energy of the room. Some people want vibrant rooms, and others respond to peaceful spaces. Being organized clears up the space for you to focus on other things. What does your perfect room look like?

Many people practice feng-shui, the art of arranging a room so that the energy can flow in a positive direction. You will feel and respond to this open, freeing peace when you enter the space. Used items you buy at a yard sale have their owners imprint on them. Sense how an item *feels* to you before bringing it into your space. Does it hold rage, stagnation, love or joy? Intend they be cleansed of all negative energy.

Evidence of energy creation exists everywhere, and yet people are still amazed when they can witness its effect. One common occurrence is for Students to have a passing thought of a friend they have not talked to in some time.

Usually, before long, the phone rings and it is their friend calling. The flow of their thought reached their companion, and they called. As simple as that.

Tyler's friend, Gillian, was fighting cancer, and the prognosis was not what they had hoped. He began to feel fear, sadness and worry. What he did not yet understand was that he was creating those energies and directing those thoughts at Gillian. She was on the receiving end. Most likely, other people, too, suffered through those same emotions as they learned of her illness.

With as many as fifty people sending Gillian fear, anxiety and sorrow as she tried to deal with her illness, she felt depleted.

If those same fifty people had focused positive thoughts towards Gillian, like love, gratitude and the sheer joy of having her in their lives, she would have been on the receiving end of uplifting strength. She would then have had more positive strength to focus on healing or to support her if the time had come to graduate from Earth School.

Acknowledge your human feelings and accept them as part of your Earth School experience. This is what it feels like to be sad, worried and fearful. Then, empower yourself with the strength of your soul. For every one frightening thought, emote two positive thoughts of love, light and encouragement to balance what you are creating. If you feel too fragile to compensate for the anxious energy, just say, "These are not my intended thoughts." Then ask your Angel for help in accomplishing what you intend.

When I was young, my father died after fighting cancer for six weeks. My anguish consumed me and yet, surprisingly, life continued. Over the next forty years, when my father came to mind, the first thing I thought about was how he died. What was unsettling was the fact that I did not contemplate the fifty years he lived, only the six weeks he suffered and died. I had become a conduit for the flow of grief and loss. No matter how hard I tried, I could not stay in the positive focus of his life. However, my intention was to stop being the conduit for negative energy, and I set out to change what I did not wish to be. I decided that for every thought I had of loss and grief, I would consciously think of two positive things my father had created with his life. I intended that the first one offset the negative thoughts and the second one move me forward in a meaningful way.

This action helped me retrain my impulse to allow shock and sorrow to define our relationship. It helped me heal and feel in control of what I was creating with my life experience. I stopped being the conduit for suffering.

Time can dull the sharp edge of pain, but what you do with the pain and time, determines the acquisition of wisdom or bitterness.

Many of us tend to remember the one negative out of one hundred positive experiences. That one occurrence can have the power to negate all the constructive influences in our lives, because it has such a sharp edge to it. If you hug a child one thousand times, and slap them once in anger, they will remember the slap. This shocking assault to their spirit can change their perception of the world and themselves.

If you are having a difficult time, wear a beloved's sweater, and you will feel comforting energy. Not all sweaters would have the same effect. If you were attending a formal affair, would you prefer to wear Princess Diana's favorite dress or one sewn by enslaved children? Would you rather wear a jacket worn by Abe Lincoln or the man who murdered him?

Positive energy has a definite course and purpose. Depending on how you manage yours, it can flow or stagnate. If you have too many conflicting thoughts, you will live in confusion.

How do you suppose the Universe will respond to these thoughts from one person?

"I wish I had time to go on a real vacation—I hope I don't forget to buy catsup when I get to the market later —I wonder if I will get that raise—Why does he comb his hair that way—My shoes are killing me, I should have bought the other pair—This is my last donut, and then I'm going to lose 10 pounds—That guy looked at me funny—I wish my nose was smaller—I can't seem to

remember anything anymore, I'm worried I'm getting senile—My rent is too high—I wish I had time to relax—I wonder what's on TV tonight?"

... Or ...

"It is my intent to learn all I can today."

My life journey brought me a daughter, born to me in my 21st year. As I helped her grow, she provided me with many learning opportunities, and in turn, she helped me expand my knowledge. Major events may change our lives and ways of thinking, but the everyday simple lessons are invaluable.

My daughter's sense of clarity is priceless. I first realized her gift when she was just two years old. We lived in a rural area, and our mailbox was three miles down a dirt road. One time when I stopped to get the mail, I accidentally locked the van door behind me. As the door shut, I realized I had just locked the keys inside with my little girl who was buckled in her car seat. I had no way to get to her. My mind went straight to panic. Should I break the window with a rock? Which window? Would she be showered in glass if I did? I remember walking around the van many times repeating, "Oh, my gosh!"

Somehow, she reached her little hand up to her window and knocked on it to get my attention. She said,

"Hey Mommy, do you want me to roll down the window?"
She unbuckled her car seat belt, jumped to the floor and
with both hands began to crank down the window.
Clarity. She didn't let the momentum of the moment
cloud her clarity.

Years later, my daughter, now grown into adulthood,
still provides me with opportunities to witness her clarity.

Two years into writing this book, I realized I had
written a total of forty pages. After two years of hard work
and time spent, how could it only be forty pages? I called
her to share my disillusionment. As I complained, she
listened, and then simply said, "Hey Mom, maybe the
book is supposed to be forty pages."

Clarity. I was wasting my time and focus, getting upset
over what might be exactly as it should be.

I am grateful for this positive energy my daughter
contributes. I know that the ways I can still contribute to
her, add to the positive energy of her life as well. For
example, I always look forward to visiting her and usually
stay for a week at a time.

I like to lend a hand with the pile of laundry that is
inevitable in most families. When I sort through the
clothes, I am always touched by my grandson's shirts, the
sundress my granddaughter loves or my daughter's
sweaters. I feel so grateful they are in my life and enjoy
being able to help with chores.

Many times, my daughter mentions that although I use
the same detergent, fabric softener, washing machine,
and dryer that she does, the clothes I wash feel better than
when she launders them. The difference we realized was

the loving energy I generated as I touched the clothes.
That energy stayed in and on the laundry. She can feel it.

The same would hold true if food were made with anger and resentment, or chores done in rage. Once energy is created, it continues.

Here are more examples of how energy transmission affects the vibration of items:

In the 1960's, the First Lady of the United States, Jacqueline Kennedy, exemplified grace and dignity. When she crossed over many years later, her family auctioned off some of her personal items, such as books she had read, pieces of jewelry and clothing. Everything she had touched was treated as valuable. Just as movies, television shows or music played in your home releases energy and settles onto everything, her thoughts, words and actions surrounded her belongings.

People will pay hard-earned money for a used napkin on which a famous person wiped his hands. A t-shirt worn by an admired singer, worth nothing in and of itself, is considered valuable, simply because that celebrity touched it with their energy.

When people visit the prison camps of Nazi Germany, they feel the anguish of the prisoners and cruelty of the guards who are now long gone. The power of torment was so strongly ingrained, that it remains.

If you were offered the chance to drink from the same cup Mother Teresa or Hitler used, which one would you choose? Would it matter to you?

What kind of energy would you feel if you held these items as I described them to you? Elvis wore these sunglasses. Babe Ruth used this bat. A rapist wore this shirt. Maya Angelou signed this book. A man was murdered on this couch. The energy generated does matter. You can feel it in your bones and sense it with your soul. Try to remember this as you live and create with your life.

Words are one of our major ways of communicating with each other. They also contain powerful energy and can encourage, deplete, empower, wound, heal, enrage, relieve, dismiss and embrace. One word can change everything. Some people allow words to tumble from their mouths, without being mindful of what they create. That is a waste of spirit and forms one's life in a careless manner.

You have the power to choose your language, the tone in which you speak, and the inflection and passion you put into your words. One kind expression of encouragement can heal a wounded soul. One nasty remark can injure a person for a lifetime. Discover the timing of when to express yourself and when to be quiet. Choose words wisely.

Communicating also involves becoming an attentive listener, so that you can truly hear what is being expressed. Only then can you respond in truth to what the other person has said.

Often, responses are mere reactions to what you think the other person is conveying. A common miscommunication results when one person says one thing, and the receiving person hears something different. This is a result of not listening, not clearly communicating, or both.

Music as a form of energy has always been part of the Universe. It frames your memories and is the backdrop to your experiences. The Earth Campus is filled with the vibrancy of rap, rock, opera, country, lullabies, classical music, jazz and more. Each one brings forth different types of energy.

Music can engage the spirit, lift the soul, open the heart, heal wounds, give a voice to your inner feelings, express your thoughts, and encourage your body to move and dance. It might also enrage the spirit with a repetitive chant of demeaning lyrics, and project a future of doom and gloom when it labels groups of people in hurtful ways.

Energy in all its variations fills and surrounds us the entire time we are in School. Color is another form. Each color has its own vibration and can illicit specific feelings from people.

If you design a room where everything is one color, the floor, walls and furniture, and put people in that space, they would most likely respond to the vibration of that color. If you put them in a blue room, they would most likely feel calmer and peaceful. A green area would help them heal and grow. Living in a light yellow environment would encourage them to feel joy. What do you suppose a gray space would do?

When I was a child, I lived next door to a woman who kept to herself. We called her the Beige Lady. The majority of her clothes, furniture and the outside of her house were tones of beige. The landscaping were shades of crème and ivory. Her personality was like her environment—monotone, yet pleasant. She seemed to lack vibrancy. I often wonder if she felt afraid to express herself outside of her comfort zone, or if she felt safe being neutral and perfectly happy existing in beige.

Of course, each color has many shades. Blue tones range from sky blue to midnight blue. Each shade represents a subtle change in energy vibration. Use color as a powerful tool to support you as you move forward on your journey, refining and defining your true self. You will learn more about it in the section about tools and gifts.

Whatever you produce with your energy goes out into the Universe. Whether you purposely manifest it or form it without regard is the difference between conscious living versus a life without direction or purpose. Either way, you are responsible for the energy you put into our world. The ripple effect of your vibration and flow of energy will eventually reach all of us in some way, and in turn, come back to you. Your choices and what you learn in your Classes will also become part of your soul, your Higher Self. They help determine the level on which your soul will exist once you graduate from Earth School.

Earth School

Classes

Explore its many paths

and lessons

Stretching out in front of all the Students in Earth School lies an expanse of the unknown waiting to be explored. It is called the Earth Campus. There, you delve into Classes that offer lessons in a wide array of subjects, ranging from Empathy and Gratitude, to Free Will and Endurance. To understand each subject, you expose yourself to the positive side of it, the negative side and everything in-between.

Your Classes present opportunities to learn in one lifetime on Earth what could take eons of time on a different dimension of reality. Here, you can learn physically, emotionally, mentally and spiritually, all at the same time. If you choose, you can quickly take the lessons to heart and make them innately yours. Remember the exploration of how you can examine the many sides of love from the chapter, "Promise of Earth School?"

Whatever your plan for education, you brought the parts of your soul to the Earth Campus that you chose to develop in Earth School. As noted earlier, your Higher Self has many parts, and you only send a few parts at a time to attend Earth School. For your soul to be completely Light, your Higher Self needs to gather all the wisdom and knowledge in every subject, usually a few subjects at a time.

Before your soul goes to Earth School on a quest to obtain enlightenment, most of you spent time deciding from an unlimited number of soul courses what you hope to study and in which scenario. You also choose what teachers you feel will best teach you and what environment will be most conducive to your ability to learn. Attending Classes and understanding and integrating the wisdom you gain into your soul increases its illumination.

Today, as Students reach further toward enlightenment, multi-tasking has become a necessity, hard study is most often a requirement, and extreme play can help release stress and discover new boundaries. Know that your drive and desire to become more than you are now will help you overcome any fear you have on the journey.

Earth School Campus

The Earth Campus is where you experience the curriculum you have chosen. The Creator designed, formed and dedicated Earth to the service of souls. Carefully planned to give you the best possible learning opportunities, the Earth School Campus became a place where souls could go to attend Classes, study and experience. It is an environment where you can test yourself and discover who you will become. Your presence on the Earth Campus has an impact and you are responsible for the energy created from that impact.

This Campus is where you create your life journey. Here, you and other individual souls come together for collective interaction. You live and create your own stories while sharing experiences of land, nature, civilization and history.

There are so many choices of places and ways to be, that no two Students lives are the same. Moreover, as each student makes a choice, a thought is formed and an action is carried out, the flow of the Earth's energy is affected. In this manner, this Campus is a living creation. Its environment alters and shifts in response to both its own force and the energy of what its students create.

The Campus has changed substantially since the energy flow of creation began 4.6 billion years ago. At this moment, more than 6.8 billion souls attend Earth School, each with a different curriculum and unique experiences. They are part of the continually changing creation. All the places on Earth are also breathing, growing, vibrant energies with different intents and purposes. They co-exist to form one Earth School.

The various Earth locations enhance our learning opportunities in a multitude of ways. The mountains rise high to inspire awe and to symbolize the challenge of the climb. The oceans and rivers mark the ebb and flow of time. Animals were woven in to nourish us, serve as our companions, and remind us of the circle of life. Plants added beauty to the land, while cleaning the air and providing food and dwellings for creatures of many species. Earth's splendor can elicit responses from our body, mind, emotions and soul.

In any given place, on any given day on Planet Earth, you can find the haves and the have nots, feast and famine, celebration and loneliness, all within sight of each other. Altogether, you have the prospect of experiencing every lesson imaginable.

Some Earth School Students prefer to stay and live in relative comfort and safety and experience as much as they can in one Campus location. But other students choose to enhance their experience by visiting, taking courses, or cohabiting with Students in a variety of Earth School sites.

This is an example of a student who embraces the entire planet:

Jack views the Earth as a fascinating place waiting to be discovered, and travels the Campus whenever he can. Hawaii is his destination for the beauty, fun and peace of spirit he feels there. Cruising on the Pacific Ocean along the coast of Alaska provides a visual feast of water lapping against frozen tundra, caribou, spouting whales and seals that share the landscape.

One unforgettable night, he observed the Northern Lights vacillating across the night sky. When he walked the streets of Rome in leather sandals, he considered who had walked there before him. The canals of Venice, a city built on water, left him marveling at human creativity. He experiences as much as he can from each new Campus location.

I encourage you to stretch yourself by taking advantage of field trips to other locations on the planet and exploring what they have to offer in the way of course study. They are an excellent way to gather knowledge. You can learn from different societies and cultures and gain valuable insights.

Unexpected Tests. Wherever you reside, the Earth Campus provides you with unexpected tests of character, soul and courage. Remember that life in Earth School is simply an opportunity to grow. Embrace the element of surprise. Will you earn to stand strong if you have never fallen? How will you learn compassion if you have not been hurt? Can you learn to be generous if no one is in need? The true test of character is not always in the tests you prepare for, but in the unexpected ones.

Just as the Earth is in a constant state of change, so is the weather that surrounds it. Unexpected weather can result in natural disasters. The point is to learn to view them as opportunities to experience something new, to further define yourself as you gather knowledge. Hurricanes, floods, tornadoes and droughts can be difficult events for Earth School Students to face. What these challenges can provide is the chance to test your courage and resolve or to rebuild anew on all levels of your Being.

Physically, you might build a new structure. Emotionally, you might be reminded of what is important. Mentally, you can amplify your resilience by discovering you are capable of navigating a difficult situation. Spiritually, you may recognize that every experience, challenging or easy, is temporary, and no matter what, you will go on. You also have the opportunity to be grateful for what you have each moment and thankful for the present moment that begins again.

Plan well or as best as you can to prepare for the unexpected. Tests pop up all the time and are a good thing, even when you don't recognize this at the time. You can gauge what you have learned by how you react to an unexpected challenge. Use it as an opportunity to become stronger than before.

Be responsible to your Campus. Beauty lives all around you and can stimulate the positive energy of your soul. However, you are on the Earth Campus at a pivotal time. The planet has become unhealthy, because the Students have not properly cared for it. Environmental problems require immediate attention. If while attending Classes here, you use too much, waste the Earth's resources, or create a cluttered and dirty environment, you damage the natural world. If you build toxic machines, dump waste in the waterways, or do not dispose of your trash appropriately, you are responsible for the resulting mess.

If you let greed guide your energy, rather than the betterment of all, what will your soul and the Campus look like when you leave? As you move forward on your journey, remain mindful of your impact.

If you can leave the Earth Campus healthier with your choices and actions, you will create a more positive environment, not only for yourself, but for everyone. Imagine an enlightened land inhabited by enlightened souls. Until then, do the absolute best you can on the Earth Campus, and then do a tiny bit more.

We are citizens of the Earth and with that citizenship arises a responsibility we need to embrace. Be a positive force on the Earth Campus. Reclaim the health of the Earth and reverse damage to the best of your ability. Imagine a new phase of Earth where we influence all in a positive light.

Teachers

Teachers appear in all the areas of your life, in many shapes, sizes and ages. Siblings, parents, families, friends, strangers and fellow workers can present you with valuable Classes in Understanding, Free Will, Sharing, claiming Personal Space and choosing your own life and path.

Some teachers will appear helpful, while others might oppose you, giving you the opportunity to strengthen your resolve to move forward. Be grateful for teachers and try to surround yourself with those who bring out the best in you—those who encourage and support you through the work you came to do. Some teachers will help you to define what you do not wish to be. They all present lessons and quiz you along the way.

Your learning is enhanced by sharing the Earth Campus with Students from every level of enlightenment and shadow. Difficult Classes can be presented by Students whose soul is stained and dim. They are opportunities to improve your fortitude and integrity.

Earth School offers a wonderful blend of serious Students, introverts and extroverts, students who support and curmudgeons who love to complain. Whatever their current status of soul growth, the majority of the Students on the Earth Campus came to School to gain strength, wisdom and understanding. A number of souls in Earth School have no plan or agenda. They have much in common with students at a university who have undeclared majors.

You also have helpers, guides, advisors, friends and counselors on the Earth Campus, and those who assist you here from the spiritual realm. They are here specifically to help you flourish in your courses. Just ask.

Many of you do remember to ask for counsel from people around you, souls who have gone before you, and from Angels and Spirit Guides. However, you will also find it useful to ask what level of light those helpers who offer aid are on before allowing it. Potential guidance may come from soul groups on either the higher or the lower levels of the spiritual realm. Before considering guidance, remember to ask, "Are you in the Light? If not, then you must go."

Another way to tell the difference is to contemplate the quality of the advice. An Advisor on the lower levels will most likely give you shady advice. Whereas, an Advisor on the highest level of light will respond with your highest good in mind. What you do with that advice is up to you.

A portion of what you learn in Classes involves determining who will support you in developing your potential and in recognizing who will try to stand in your way. When do you need help and when do you stand up for yourself? Who can you call for advice or just to listen? Who will encourage you to move forward, and who will entice you to drop out? Who will nurture you and who drains you? Under what circumstances do you feel comfortable or lost? When do you decide to move forward on a path, and when do you stop, reverse direction or take a different path? Guidance is always available to you, day or night, if you just ask. No appointment is necessary and it is free of charge.

Soul Classes Offered In Earth School

Twelve years ago, a young couple came to see me. They were expecting a child. The baby's soul, Jackson, had important information to share with his future parents. Paying close attention, I stayed aligned with God, while Jackson began to show me his intentions. He was coming to Earth not only to attend his Classes, but also to participate in helping humanity come together with the understanding we are one world, not divided. Timing and education were important for this to happen.

Jackson appeared to me in his future body at the age of thirty. He was tall, fit, focused and well educated. He was currently sitting in a higher energetic level in the company of enlightened souls who were offering their wisdom. Carefully planning his Earth School education, he was contemplating taking the Classes of Tolerance, Knowledge, Balance and Integrity.

As his parents took notes, Jackson showed me he was choosing specific genes from his biological family. This was the most carefully planned Earth School curriculum I have witnessed. First, he chose his mother's wisdom of life, his father's ability to learn, his maternal grandmother's openness, his paternal grandmother's tenacity and his paternal grandfather's patience. He continued through aunts and cousins, uncles and distant relatives, choosing what he felt would serve him well.

Although his relatives are short in stature, he reached back into his genetic pool and pulled forth the gene that would allow him to grow to six feet or more. He felt that having a strong presence was important.

Next, he wanted his parents to know his soul essence was that of Light, and he was determined to live a life of purpose. He had chosen his mother specifically for her ability to guide and provide him with the stimulation his brain would need to grow beyond average capability. She was already playing classical music for him, talking to him, eating well and maintaining a positive state of Being. This was helping him develop more neural pathways in his brain. Once he was born, Jackson desired to be a person of integrity with strong morals and he intended to gather knowledge daily.

I remember a day when Jackson was five years old. Riding in the back seat of the car, he was concerned he hadn't learned anything that day. His grandmother pointed out the window and talked about the clouds, air currents and the birds soaring in the wind. Then she told him about the importance of having a quiet mind, being content in the moment and knowing there is always something to be learned. Jackson wanted more.

Asking his baby sister if she wanted to learn something, she said, "No, I'm good." She was part of his life to provide him with the opportunity to learn balance and tolerance.

This year, at the age of 11, he received several academic awards and a medal from his teacher for kindness. Jackson also received a certificate from an Ivy League University for Academic Talent Recognition. It offered him possibilities for scholarships.

His plans and intentions before coming to the Earth Campus are now a reality. It is now up to him to stay the course, re-adjust when necessary, and live his life in the best way possible.

Jackson is aware of problems in his school, society and the planet, and is interested in solutions to help this world be a better, more affable place for a soul to grow. After all, that's what he came here to do.

How many Classes did you decide to attend? Here are more examples of lessons and opportunities as they appear on the Earth Campus:

JoAnne and Beth met in kindergarten and became immediate friends. However, their home lives were very different. Beth had two parents who provided a loving home and were financially comfortable. Life for Beth was steady and predictable.

JoAnne had a hard-working, loving mother and absent alcoholic father. She started working at an early age to help with the bills at home and developed a strong work ethic. Her time after school was booked with babysitting, dog walking, and house cleaning—whatever job was offered to her. JoAnne built a reputation in town for being reliable and enchanting.

During their high school years, JoAnne was kept busy with her many jobs. Beth pursued her passion for horses and became an accomplished barrel racer. One year, she was crowned Rodeo Queen at the County Fair. Beth was able to pursue her life without the struggle or stress that JoAnne experienced daily.

Having watched them both grow up I wondered if JoAnne ever felt envious of Beth. When I asked her, she looked at me bewildered and said, "Why would I be jealous of my friend?"

I replied, "Because Beth seems to have an easier life, and you carry a heavy load." Again, she looked at me curious that I would say such a thing. Then JoAnne asked, "What could Beth have learned?" At her young age of 14, JoAnne understood the value of Earth School. She expected to be challenged and tested to push her to grow as a person and a soul.

Beth and JoAnne had come to Earth School with different curriculums. Lessons that appeared in their lives were Classes to present them with information in the area of their chosen study.

In reality, fair and unfair does not apply to the learning process. Each lesson is unique in order to provide for individual needs. Even it two souls attend the same course they will experience two separate lessons that relate to what they chose to learn.

Like JoAnne, consider what challenges you in your life and view it as a lesson from which to learn.

When you accept your life as a learning opportunity, every moment has value and meaning. Give yourself permission to live the best life you possibly can. You will not get a second chance to live the same moment.

Fiona and Mia both came to Earth School to learn compassion—as many sides to it as they could—the meaning, focus, lack and fullness of this complex subject. This is their story:

Mia was born beautiful and healthy. Her mother, Fiona, was grateful for the exquisite gift of a child. The first few nights Mia slept well and only woke to be fed and changed, then went right back to sleep. That peace didn't last when Mia developed colic. Fiona worried, walked the floor, called the doctor and changed Mia's diet. Still the baby cried day and night for weeks, with no end in sight.

Fiona thought she was going to lose her mind. She tried to focus on compassion for Mia—if she would just stop crying! There were moments she lost her temper with the baby, cried with her, laid her down or walked away for a few minutes. Her compassion was tested further than she thought she could go, but Fiona did it, even when she wanted to give in to her frustration. She said out loud, "I choose compassion for my daughter. She is helpless in her pain. I am so grateful to have her." Even though she failed sometimes, Fiona intended gratitude to guide her life and she became stronger than anger and frustration. Mia was seven months old when her colic began to recede.

Eighty years later, Fiona and Mia left the doctor's office, hand in hand. He had delivered the challenging diagnosis of Alzheimer's. Fiona's brain was withering. She was losing her memory and control of her emotions. The daughter worried, sat with her mother, called specialists and changed Fiona's diet hoping for a cure. But her mother began to cry uncontrollably and became unreasonable.

Mia knew her mother was in emotional and mental pain, and there were moments Mia thought she would lose her mind. There were times she lashed back at her mother and instances she cried with her. Then she made a conscious choice to cling to compassion with everything she had, and love rose to the surface, making the suffering more bearable.

During moments of clarity, Fiona experienced loss of control and tried to be gracious in accepting help from other people. Mia gradually realized that her mother's illness was an opportunity for soul growth for many people. Everyone involved with Fiona's care was faced with different challenges, and each of them had the free will to react to the test in the way they chose.

In their lifetime together, mother and daughter learned Compassion in many forms and unexpectedly learned several lesson in the subject of Gratitude. When they thought they had reached their limits, they each made a conscious choice to push further, even when they didn't feel it. They intended and repeated it until it became their truth.

Keep in mind the difference between surviving and thriving. You can choose between just getting through the immediate moment and true learning. This involves recognizing the lesson and its teaching, taking it to heart and integrating it into your soul. When you accomplish that, the lesson becomes part of your wisdom and inherent knowledge.

Mateo is a busy man, a good man, but his life was full of noise. Working at the New York Stock Exchange did not give him a moment of peace, and his family provided non-stop commotion at home. He added to the noise by leaving the television on when he wasn't paying attention to it. It had become normal for his mind to chatter continually.

He was not aware of it until we talked, but his soul was in Earth School to learn about the subjects of Peace, Silence and Self Value. As a young man, Mateo had been most content when he was hiking and could just be. Now his soul was crying out to be heard.

As his life took on more responsibility, there had been little time to pursue his need for tranquility. Mateo said he was ready to change what he could, but he wasn't in the position to move to a mountaintop and meditate all day.

This is what he decided to do with the advice we were shown. If he couldn't become quiet, he would intend for his Being to become aware and peaceful. If he could not become silent, he could practice silence. Maybe not conquer, but practice silence. The more he practiced, the more he realized his mind was becoming content. Then, his emotions became calm. His spirituality began to flourish, and his physical body relaxed. He was well on his way to exploring his courses on many levels.

What you learn in each of your Classes depends on your individual need and choice. Consider the subject of Endurance. First, you would learn the meaning of endurance, then the positive qualities, the negative features, and all the aspects in between. You learn when to endure something and when to endure it no more. You can watch other people endure difficult situations and learn from observing. Will you help them endure, encourage them to stop enduring or ignore them?

Eve lives in a lovely apartment near Lake Michigan. Today is her 94th birthday. She woke up early to dust and clean. By lunchtime, she is ready to watch her favorite soap operas and rest.

She takes pride in her appearance and dresses nicely each day, adding a piece or two of jewelry. People tell her she doesn't look a day over seventy, which pleases her.

One morning a week, Eve's neighbor drives her to the grocery store, and she buys her husband's favorite foods. Then, she cooks his breakfast, so that it is ready when he wakes up at noon. Because he can be grumpy and difficult, she takes care not to say anything that might upset him. Most days, she fails.

Eve was deeply influenced by her generation's judgment that marriage is forever, even if it becomes unhealthy and toxic. As a result, for their sixty years of marriage, Eve has been her husband's servant and victim. He belittles her over the smallest of circumstances. He does not even eat at the kitchen table with her. For the last twenty years, he has chosen to watch sports on TV while he eats.

When Eve had a party for her 60th birthday, her husband ruined it by yelling at her. She told her niece, who had come to the event, "If I was only ten years younger, I would leave him and create a peaceful life. But if I leave, no one else would take care of him."

"Maybe if he had to take care of himself, he might change his attitude," her niece replied.

On her 70th birthday, Eve told her cousin, "If I were ten years younger, I would leave this horrible relationship."

On her 80th birthday, Eve called her brother and said, "If I were only ten years younger, I wouldn't put up with his abuse and would get a little apartment by myself."

On her 90th birthday, guess what she told her sister, "if only" . . .

Eve is attending Earth School Classes in Self Worth, Joy, Love and Endurance. When her soul rises up to another dimension, she hopes to find value in what she perceives to be mistakes, as well as good decisions, because mistakes can be valuable lessons too, as long as you learn from them.

Eve's soul had hoped for a lifetime of social interaction and a warm, supportive family. Instead, she abandoned her personal life journey to accompany her husband on his path. She gave up her family, because they eventually refused to be around him. She feared being lonely if she left. But in reality, loneliness would have been a small challenge compared to her lifetime of allowing herself to be a victim.

Learning to face conflict and not ignore it takes strength and courage, but if you deal with it immediately and directly, you can save yourself a lifetime of struggle. Each is a lesson unto itself.

I strongly advise you to review your life journey regularly. If your life, work, health choices, or relationships are not working well, you would be wise to make some changes.

The courses you signed up for today may not serve you the rest of your life. What if you found one of them did not meet your needs, or you chose not to accept the teacher heading the course? Today, Students realize they can change their soul journey and are not stuck taking Classes that are no longer in their highest good. In other words, what moved you forward when you were eighteen years old might not serve you when you are forty. Imagine how much more knowledge can be gained in a lifetime when you can adjust your life and guide your encounters moment to moment. Your intention will open the door for positive change in your life.

One of my courses is Abandonment. During my lifetime, I have left relationships that did not work for me and also had my heart broken by being left behind. Many hours have been spent sitting with people who are feeling abandoned and observing rejection. This subject has been a big part of my life.

Several years ago, I experienced one of the most painful abandonments in my life. I just couldn't take this

Class anymore. I was angry, living in sorrow, and felt I could not continue to be involved in this course for one more day. I refused to participate in Abandonment ever again.

That night I intended that when I went to sleep, my astral soul would go up to my Higher Self and change my curriculum. I invited Advisors and Guides in the Highest Light, who could give me suggestions, counseling, direction—anything that would help me drop the course. Nothing was going to sway me. I was determined to delete the lesson completely and change it to Joy or Harmony Class.

When I woke up in the morning, I was surprised to feel peaceful, content and more in tune with my Being. However, despite my strong intention, the unexpected happened. I was stunned to find I still had my Class in Abandonment.

Although I didn't consciously remember what happened that night with my Higher Self, I do know I came away from the meeting knowing I had almost accomplished enough in the subject to be complete in that area—illuminated, but not quite fully enlightened. The understanding I woke with was similar to realizing I was a junior in college and had already gained wisdom that would make my senior year easier than the years before.

Did I want to quit now? My informed choice was to continue. With that knowing, I was now content to do so.

Many souls do complete their original Earth School courses and line up new lessons to take. Or, they discover they are far enough along with their course study that they can handle additional Classes. Some souls bring in new lessons as they feel ready for them. Others made arrangements before they were born for a new course to come to their astral soul if they attained a certain level of education or age. The possibility of learning multiplies when you incorporate this flexibility.

Check in with your soul often and make adjustments in your Class load as you see fit. If you proceed with a course, instead of shifting to the path you now realize is better for you, you could be in danger of wasting your energy on something that will not matter to you in the end. The decision is yours.

Remember to stretch. That includes your body, mind, emotions and spirit

One life lesson I have learned is to make my choices mindfully. That way, I stretch myself and live the life I choose, not a passive life that happens to me randomly. I have to remind myself that I can change myself or my perspective, alter it, be comfortable with it, or endure it. It is my choice. Here are some more of the unexpected lessons I have learned in Earth School.

- Your learning experience will be different from mine, even if we attend the same Class.

- Take nothing personally. Everything that happens can be viewed as a Class. If you can view all experiences as having a teaching and learning purpose, you will have a clearer perception of your soul journey.

- Don't forget your tools when you go to Class. Some of them are in the gifts of Spirit—like intuition, Angelic support, intention and free will. Practice using your tools so they become second nature.

- Some Classes you will seem to fail, and others you will pass, thereby gaining their wisdom. In truth, failure can be a Class in itself. Learn from it.

- What is worse than staying in a toxic Class for ninety days? The answer is staying in the Class for ninety days and one minute.

- Realize that pretending to be different than what you are harms everyone. Speak your truth, even if others don't understand. The world needs you to be you. You are the only one who can complete your schooling.

- Lessons are learned as much, if not more, from hard experiences as from easy ones. Deal with them as directly and as positively as you can.

- You cannot get something from another Student or teacher if they do not have it to give.

- You have the choice to rise above negativity or to sink into it.

- Everything you have ever done prepares you for all that you can do and be.

- Let this be the time you release your fears about what you can achieve.

- Know what you want and be willing to give yourself what you need to live the best life you possibly can.

Enjoy your time in School. Celebrate yourself and all those you encounter.

Angels

Light Beings of Grace

Messengers of Hope

Lift your eyes and see what is

Aspire to be more – I will help you

The loveliest part of working as a Soul Advocate is meeting Angels. Most often, when I begin a session, I ask to see the client's Guardian Angel. This assures truth, protection and Light for our conversation and facilitates a closer bond between the individual soul and their Guardian Angel.

Early on in my work, before I spoke to people about their Angels, I felt it was necessary for me to understand the creation of Angels and the way in which they interfaced with us. Here is what I experienced: Imagine a luminous ball of Light. Sparks spring from the Light, separating and moving outward. As each spark separates from the radiant ball, a beam of Light, that stays connected to the sphere and is no different from it, follows the spark wherever it goes. The spark is a soul. The beam of Light is a Guardian Angel, and the glowing ball is the Creator.

We are the spark of God's Light, and our Guardian Angel is a beam of that Light, fully connected to the Creator, yet responding to us. Angels are not separate from the Creator, but are an extension of God. They are like a hand reaching down from the source of Light from which souls are created. These Beings of Grace are an expression of The Great Spirit's energy. They stretch from Him to wherever they are needed. This is how God is in every place, in every moment, with every soul. Light Beings of Grace are present, yet non-intrusive, to allow our free will. They are always standing by us in Earth School as we discover our true self and explore our opportunities.

Know that you are never alone. Even if you cannot see anything in front of you, Angelic Messengers of Hope are with you to love and assist in the most positive way possible. You may feel their support in your soul or sense it with your body. They can provide you with tools, guidance and encouragement as you create your life, attend your Classes and learn to expand the Light in your soul.

Your Guardian Angel manifests with a specific appearance, personality and mannerisms that are perfect for your partnership and interaction. Many Angels are seen as a vision of diffused Light for ease and beauty. An Angel, who promotes truth seeking and simplicity, can take the form of an apostle. A person, who leaves chaos behind in his or her wake, might have a Guardian Angel that resembles a cleaning lady. Theatrical Angels grab your attention, and graceful Angels glide on water to encourage the flow in your life.

Guardian Angels can take the energetic form of a fisherman, symbolizing the seeking and capture of wisdom. Other Angels may take the form of a Sumo wrestler to serve those souls that might be prone to fear or living a life that would benefit from strong security. A Guardian Angel like that can clear energy with one enormous shake.

Guardian Angels

As each soul is uniquely created, so is an Angel unlike any other. This Being of Grace reaches from God to stand alongside the spark that is your soul and remains with you throughout time. I call these Beings your Guardian Angels. Some call them Spirit Guides, Helpers, or Light Beings.

There are many names for this extension of the Creator's Light.

Our Guardian Angel is, in fact, a gift so brilliant that you may find it difficult to comprehend. We have received this gift for a reason. Guardian Angels are with us since the moment we come into Being. This will not change while we are in Earth School.

They are not only our helpers, but also our partners. They know exactly what we expect to accomplish and how we hope to achieve our goal. That understanding is present because we share our goals with them before coming to Earth School. On the Earth Campus, they are more important to us than ever. They are with us for many reasons.

One job of our Guardian Angels is to shield the glow of the Spark of our soul, while encouraging it to expand. Imagine, if you would, a campfire. It begins as a spark. If you put small bits of twigs and paper and blow gently on it, you breathe life into it, and it will grow. There are times to tend the fire with delicate care and times to let it burn. Too much kindling, and it can smother. Not enough, and it struggles to stay aglow. When the wind gusts are strong, you need to stand between the storm and the Spark to guard and shelter the flame. You gauge how fast it should grow and monitor the flame from raging out of control. If that occurred, all its energy might be consumed and dwindle to embers.

The partnership between our Guardian Angel and our soul is similar in nature to the campfire. As souls, we begin as a Spark of Light. Guardian Angels are Protectors to keep that Spark viable and growing. They tend to our small breath of life, blowing gently on it as it grows bigger and brighter. They gather up little bits of opportunities and lessons, and present them to us to encourage our Spark to grow into a strong, steady flame. If our soul Light is ever in danger of dimming from an excess of adversity, sorrow, or negativity, our Angel shields and buffers it from being overwhelmed.

Angels also help to prevent our soul Light from blazing out of control. The human body can have a difficult time trying to contain a soul Light that is shooting energy in erratic directions and is not maintaining equilibrium. With our permission, our Angel will support us to stay in balance.

Here are a few more services your Angel provides:

Partner And Guide
A strong presence to lean on ~ Strength to lift you
Just ask

Guardian Angels are tools to assist us in our spiritual journey. However, a tool is only useful if we use it. They are truly our perfect counselor for on the spot and long-term advice and direction. Angels will never command us.

Kim is a student on the Earth Campus who deals with disabling physical and mental fatigue. She was diagnosed many years ago with Chronic Fatigue Syndrome. Doctors are able to offer Kim palliative care, but not a cure. Kim frequently feels so out of control with her pain and exhaustion that she tries to focus on where she can exert a measure of control. She meticulously organizes her material items—bills, pictures, dishes and clothes are stored in strict order. This organizing behavior calms and empowers her.

Seven is her Guardian Angel. He determined the best way to help Kim was by organizing his partnership with her. First, he communicated with her through her clairsentient ability. Next, he wrapped seven boxes in the most beautiful coverings and lined them up in front of him. Since Kim finds it difficult to concentrate on more than one thing at a time, Seven opens just one box at a time. The energy in the selected box flows around Kim in a manner that is comfortable and useful to her.

The first box is wrapped in glacier blue, tied with iridescent gold ribbon. It contains the energy of compassion. Most of the time, Kim is without support or encouragement from another soul, as her illness has isolated her. Yet, when Seven opens this box, Kim feels compassion and receives companionship from a greater source. It gives her strength to continue her journey.

The second box is sunrise yellow with silver bells on top. This box contains the power of joy. When Seven lifts the top off this box, the bells chime with the loveliness of joy. The energy encircles Kim, encouraging her to be joyful in the present moment.

The third box is the rich green color of thick island moss. It holds the energy of growth and nurturing. This encourages Kim to research and learn all she can about the condition of her life. With this knowledge, she can decide what to keep or discard. This inspires her entire Being.

The fourth box is covered in peach velvet with tinges of yellow and baby green. Tenderness emanates from within this gift. Kim's soul is growing with this energy to benefit not only her, but all souls. This gift connects her to the love of Spirit.

Soft indigo Light forms the fifth box. It represents the vibrancy of wholeness, reminding Kim that she is complete unto herself. In this completeness, she is part of the Unity of all Souls.

The white box is comprised of ringlets of Light. Seven calls it the 911 gift. When Kim feels overwhelmed, he brings this box to rest in Kim's hands. In that moment, she is holding the strength of her true self. This box empowers her to reach out, encouraging her to accept support from outside of her comfort zone.

The last gift is silver satin tied with white ribbon, edged in glimmer. This box represents wisdom and is filled with the knowledge Kim has gathered in her lifetime. When she feels meaningless or falters, this box is a gift to validate her importance. It also reminds her how far she has come and inspires her to persevere in her journey.

Seven knows when to open a box and when to close one, all in Kim's highest good. His partnership with Kim has been honed to a fine art. Here is an example of how they work together:

Last year, Kim became gravely ill and drove herself to the emergency room at the local hospital. She carefully gave the staff her medical information. The hospital admitted her and put her in a patient room on the third floor.

Several hours passed, and the nurses neglected to give her the medication she needed. Kim requested it repeatedly, until she became so upset that the hospital staff ignored her altogether.

Feeling hopeless, she curled up and began to cry softly. Seven picked up the white box that contains 911 energy and placed it in Kim's hands.

A wave of courage swept through Kim. She reached for the phone and called 911 from her hospital bed. The operator could not understand why someone would call for emergency assistance when they were already in the hospital. Kim calmly explained that if she did not get her medicine immediately, she could die. Again, the 911 operator explained that they could not send an emergency crew to a hospital patient. It was then that Kim said, "At least there would be a record of my call explaining my situation." The operator brought her supervisor into the conversation and together they called the hospital administrator to inform him of Kim's dilemma.

Kim had her medication within the hour, and changes were implemented to the procedures and staff at the hospital. Kim is proud that she stood up for herself that day and hopes the changes at the hospital will benefit other patients.

The 911 gift from Seven turned into a 911 call for help that brought about the medical attention that Kim needed.

Stand on the Path You Are Hoping to Take And Get Your Attention
A thought ~ A symbol to guide you ~ Tulips in winter Did you see it?

Our Guardian Angels will remind us why we came to Earth School. They will stand on the path of our highest good and get our attention. Watch for signs and symbols. Do not just ask and ask again. Remember to listen, watch, and wait, with all of your senses for guidance. Be silent in your soul, voice and mind.

Do not be like the man on the rooftop when the water was rising. He was so sure that help would come from God in the way *he* imagined that he did not recognize assistance when it arrived.

Whether related to a job, relationship, location, illness or classroom, *just ask*. If you pay attention, information will be placed in front of you to guide you on the path for the highest good of your soul. You have the free will to take the advice or disregard it.

Paul was proud to be a truck driver. He had driven big rigs since he was old enough to get his license. He had made a decent living, and his wife and children enjoyed their home in a friendly community.

In the past few years, the cost of living had risen substantially, more than any raises or bonuses he had managed to earn. Consequently, his paycheck did not go as far as it once did, and the bills were piling up. Paul had a decision to make. He would have to look for a second job or find a better paying position.

He began scanning the job boards at the truck stops he frequented and got the word out that he was looking for a better opportunity. It did not take long before he received a job offer from a company based in Alabama. So much to consider. It would mean uprooting his family and starting over in a new state. Initially, that would be hard on everyone. He was losing sleep, trying to decide what was best for the family.

Like Paul, we all face decisions that we have to make without all the answers. My suggestion is to ask for guidance. Then, think with your mind, feel with your heart and decide with your soul.

After a month of indecision, Paul asked me to assist him in getting advice. He told me that he had been asking for clarity and felt he had been ignored. All he wanted was a sign or symbol, anything to guide him in the best direction.

Paul was clairaudient, which a gift of spiritual hearing, although he did not understand that term. It was normal for him to hear words or songs inside himself. He thought everyone did and never stopped to think it was a gift. He did not consciously realize it, but that was how his Angel spoke to him.

We talked about his gift for some time, discussing how signs and symbols can be right in front of us and somehow we don't always recognize them. His Guardian Angel, Leora, was part of our conversation, and she showed me how she had been putting many bits of information in front of Paul.

Leora knew Paul liked country music and enjoyed listening to the radio while he drove. It kept him company on his long hauls. But these days, his mind would quickly wander back to his job dilemma.

A few weeks passed before he realized that every time he thought about his situation, the song "Sweet Home Alabama" would come on the radio. Paul thought it was a strange coincidence. His Angel knew better.

Late one night, while he was fueling his truck, he saw a poster in the window of the gas station. The band Alabama was coming to the Convention Center on the weekend of his wife's birthday. He thought going to the concert would be a nice surprise and called for tickets. The Angel was instrumental in Paul spotting that poster.

In the shower, he found himself humming a song he learned when he was a kid. Most of the words eluded him, and he could not remember the name of it, something about "come from Alabama with a banjo on my knee." He had a hard time getting it out of his head. It reminded him of the happiness he experienced in his childhood.

Now, if he could just get a sign of whether or not to take that job in Alabama ...

Leora knew that the change and the people he would have the opportunity to meet on the new job in Alabama were the best circumstances for his soul journey. She stood on that path and tried to get his attention.

Now, Paul can consider his Angel's guidance or go down a different path.

Remember, easy does not mean best, and sometimes the best path is harder. Taking meaningful and significant Classes takes time and hard work. No one attended a university, rested on the lawn all day, and graduated with the capability to be an accomplished professional. Your Angel will stand on the path you are hoping to take for your highest good.

If we walk the easiest path on the Earth Campus, what will we learn? Sitting on the outside and observing the coming and going of other Students, or actively attending the Classes—which will give the greater education?

Anisa is a beautiful and intelligent woman. She has worked her way up the corporate ladder in the advertising world. This profession is usually in a constant state of change as accounts come and go. When one job closes, Anisa tries to have the next one lined up.

Judy is Anisa's Guardian Angel. She looks remarkably similar to the Statue of Liberty. I told Anisa about her Angel, and she began to notice the Statue of Liberty in many curious places. It was Judy's way of confirming to Anisa that she was with her.

Anisa became aware that her current job was most likely ending and once again, she would need to find a new one. She asked Judy to give her a sign of which path was in her highest good. Then she waited and went out on several job interviews.

One interview in particular was causing her to feel apprehensive. The CEO of the company wanted to talk with her himself. At the appointed time, Anisa was escorted into his office. The large space was impressive, with gleaming marble floors and a spectacular view of the city. Something caught her eye, and she turned to see a large green Statue of Liberty made of Lego's. The toy was so out of place that Anisa asked the CEO about it.

He explained that his six-year-old son had built it by himself. The CEO was so proud of his son's work that he brought it to work with him to display in his office that day. Another subtle sign from Judy.

Anisa considered that sign, asked intelligent questions, walked through the office to experience the environment, and then, with her soul, made the choice to accept the job.

Our Guardian Angels will try their best to get through to us. The partnership you have established with yours will determine how you interact and communicate with each other.

Omni Present

Are you with me, or am I truly alone?

Ellen watched a TV show that featured people who

claimed to receive divine intervention when there seemed to be no hope. Part of her believed, and part of her was cynical. Actually, her mind considered believing to be foolish, her heart yearned for it to be true, and her soul sat in the peace of knowing.

When she came to see me, I asked to see her Guardian Angel. Although I rarely heard with my inner gift of clairaudience, I could hear trumpets playing. With my clairvoyance, I saw a large stage framed with velvet curtains held back with gold rope. From stage left, an elaborately groomed Angel entered and announced that he was Arthur, Guardian Angel of Ellen. He had many things to share with Ellen through me. The unusual thing about Arthur was that he spoke like a Shakespearean actor. Each word voiced was an announcement.

Guardian Angels often give people who come to me for a session, confirmation of their existence after they leave and Arthur was no different. As she drove home, Ellen decided to ask for a sign from him that gave her tangible evidence. Sitting in the car, she said aloud, "If you really exist, give me a sign."

Twenty minutes later, she pulled up to her mailbox before turning into her driveway. She opened the lid and before she even put her hand on it, she saw it. The top piece of mail was from the Angel Society and printed in big red letters, it said, "Do you believe in Angels?" The second piece of mail was from her niece who had sent Ellen a new drawing to display on her refrigerator—a picture of her niece's favorite cartoon character, Arthur.

She went right into the house, called me and asked, "Do you think this is a sign?"

People can feel so lost and confused that even when they get their sign, they still question.

Give Comfort
A safe place to rest ~ An ear to listen
A sigh of release
Do you feel it?

Berta works with people in conflict. She and her Angel, Angela, are both slight of build and have soft brown hair and kind, comforting hands that belong only to the loveliest of Light. Even when she was a little girl, Berta was aware of Angela and knew that she was with her every moment helping, holding and encouraging her.

Berta is a mental health specialist with the strongest of intentions to support souls that are wounded. Her life's work has been to help others in their times of need. It did not matter what job she held, and she worked at many to support her family, she always connected with the people she met. The ability to validate others, their experiences and their dreams is in her essence.

Berta's spiritual gift of intuition is strong. She can recognize a troubled soul, a scared child or confused adult. Instinctively, her words are well chosen, her voice resonates with kindness, and her heart understands the state of another soul. I have yet to witness anyone leave her presence without having shared a laugh or smile.

One job in particular holds a special place in Berta's soul. For several years, she was a Child Advocate in an elementary school. Instead of creating an office, she fashioned a room for the children. She filled it with every sort of toy and game. Art projects lined the walls and were proudly displayed in the windows. Children would come to Berta's room when life led them to find a safe place, a friend, a helper and most importantly, someone who saw them as a valuable soul.

The peace they found in that room came from Berta's energy and her intent to help them and because Angela touched each child who entered the room. Sometimes she held them in her lap or placed her hand on their shoulder. They were directly comforted by Angelic energy. It was a partnership that accomplished what Berta had intended to create and share.

Berta once told me that the calm Angela brings, allows her to give her best. Berta is so grateful to have Angela. May you all have a Berta in your life.

Encourage You To Find
Your True Self

A nudge ~ A knowing sigh ~ A gentle reminder
A whispering of words without sound
Did you hear that?

Ella came to see me on a lark, thinking it would be great fun to have me predict her future. She was disappointed when I told her I have found the future is an unknown, because the soul has free will in every moment to decide which way to go. Sometimes, I am shown the direction of the highest probability, so the person will have as much information as possible before going down that path. More often than not, I am shown what is meant for the person to know or work through in that moment.

After getting permission, with my inner vision, I saw that Ella was surrounded by pumpkins. I didn't know what that meant and asked to see Ella's Angel. Dressed in blue from head to toe, Blanche is a sturdy little Angel, who resembles a storybook fairy godmother. However, she is not a fairy godmother—she is Ella's Guardian Angel.

Blanche told me that the pumpkins represented all the questionable men Ella had welcomed into her life. Fairytales had been compelling to Ella when she was a child, and she stringently held on to the fable that finding her perfect mate would complete her—and then she would be happy. She went on to tell me that Ella wasn't interested in much of anything else, no matter how much Blanche tried to get her attention. She was content to give all of her interest to her physical world and hadn't given much thought to her soul.

It was Ella's belief that if she kissed enough frogs, one of them would turn into her perfect mate. However, when you kiss a frog, it simply becomes a frog that has been kissed.

I could see that Ella had a gift for many things, but she had no talent for choosing a compatible partner. She was drawn to questionable characters, intending to fix them. She felt uncomfortable acknowledging her own weaknesses and finding the strength to work on them. Trying to change other people kept her distracted, so she could ignore her soul education.

Attempting to fix someone else's life can take all of your time, leaving you little or no time to walk your own journey. However, it was not in Ella's soul plan to keep being sidetracked by men who did not want to change. Since Ella is gifted with clairaudience, Blanche whispers in Ella's ear, "A pumpkin is just a pumpkin," when Ella meets yet another distraction. She simply brushes that thought aside while she looks for the next frog. Maybe now that Ella is aware of Blanche, she will listen, but meanwhile, her relationship journey is a work in progress.

I spent two hours with Ella, delivering spiritual messages that were shown to me. At the end of our talk, I asked Ella if she had any questions. She had one. "When will I meet my perfect man?" Blanche was right.

In the process of taking Classes, your Angels will encourage you to choose good over evil, and to be caring and strong rather than hurtful and mean. After you have chosen, they will help you fit all of your pieces together forming the Light of your existence.

Rush to Your Aid

A cry in the night ~ A softening of sorrow
A lifting of spirit ~ A Light in the dark ~ I am here

Angels will hold you close when you are in fear. They will also help you use your gifts to move forward, remind you of the lesson your Class is teaching you, and encourage you to be wise.

Christmas morning had always looked the same. First, Michelle was the child excited to begin the day with family and celebration. Then, she became the adult who helped to create the day.

This year would look different. Her children had started their own lives and lived far away. Her husband left their marriage soon after. Nobody would be coming home. Michelle would be dealing with her perfect picture of what Christmas was supposed to look like alone.

The panic and tears started on Christmas Eve. She could not see beyond her pain until she cried out for help. "Just help me breathe through this moment until the next one is here … and then the next one …"

A softening of sorrow began inside her. She felt a knowing she had not sensed before. "You don't have to know right now what is next. Just be. Just breathe. I am here. You are not alone. You are right where you belong. You are growing into you. These are growing pains. Everything changes. Let go of trying to control your life and show up to see what this Christmas is supposed to look like."

Michele became determined to change her perspective and let go of the perfect picture. Christmas does not have to have a tree, presents or even family. This circumstance was not the worst thing that could happen.

She told herself, "All is well. This is a lesson in Being. This is not personal. I will watch, wait and be present in this moment." Because she was fully aware, calm, willing and grateful, the day was perfect. She had everything she needed to just Be. That Christmas was simplicity and peace in its finest form.

Get Your Attention
When You Are Not Living Your Truth
A fluttering wisp of Light ~ A quickening of movement
A red flag ~ Did you see it?

Light Beings of Grace have full knowledge of everything that you have been, what you hope to achieve and how you hope to accomplish it. They remember what you have forgotten on your spiritual path and remind you at the appropriate moment. Therefore, Angels are radiance from above that help us to remember why we are here.

At 6'8" and weighing 430 pounds, Trevor was a large man. His wife scheduled an appointment for him to see me. He begrudgingly showed up at my door.

His Guardian Angel was the first thing I saw around him. Her name was April, and she appeared to be quite frustrated. April presented as a tiny cleaning lady and held an even tinier wand topped off with a little star that had sharp points. I asked April how she was able to get Trevor's attention. After all, he was so large, and she was very small. April proceeded to tap him on the left side of his head with her sharp wand. The man did not respond to my comments about his Angel until it was time for him to leave.

As Trevor was stepping out the door, he hesitated, turned around and came back. He sheepishly told me that he had been trying to figure out why he would feel a twinge on the left side of his head when he was doing something he was not proud of. He had even asked his doctor to look at it one time. Now he knows.

Protect You
Even From Yourself
Unwavering love ~ Armor of Light
Protective arms to hold you ~ Sacred strength and courage

Quintelet is a powerful Guardian Angel, fifty feet tall, with what looks to be afterburners for quick flight and expediency. He was created for Jeff and extends from the strong Protective energy of Light.

Jeff has a hazardous job and a dangerous addiction but also the intention to be a good man. He needs a Light Being who is powerful enough to shake up strong energy to get his attention.

Jeff is clairsentient. He has a gut reaction to the energy present in the moment. This is a powerful gift to feel within yourself—what feels right and what seems wrong. Quintelet uses this gift to communicate with Jeff. With each year that goes by, Jeff is beginning to acknowledge his clairsentient gift as a talent that can guide him with decisions and opportunities. However, at times Jeff still chooses to ignore his gut feeling.

Jeff works as a logger in the mountains of Northern California. He is in danger every time he enters the forest. Falling trees, rolling logs, chain saws and uneven terrain can cause things to go wrong quickly. Making a living working outdoors appeals to Jeff. He is not the kind of man who would be happy sitting behind a desk. His father was a logger, too, and Jeff followed his example. He inherited more than his love of the woods from his father. He also inherited the gene present in alcoholics. Jeff's drinking has caused problems for him and even more pain for those who love him.

Quintelet's strong protection has saved Jeff more than once from bears, beers and muddy roads. He shields Jeff, even from himself, when appropriate, while Jeff creates his life.

Divine Strength and Love

Lift your eyes and see what is
Aspire to be more ~ I will help you

Guardian Angels can stand in front of you to buffer the energy coming your way. Once you are in School, you will notice times when someone may say something mean to you, and it will feel like you have been bowled over. A week later, they might say something to you that is even harsher, and you will hardly pay attention to it. Why is that?

When you have your Angel standing in front of you, the words and energy that accompany them must first pass through the pure positive Light energy of your Angel before it touches you in any way—physically, emotionally, mentally, or spiritually. Much of the sharp energy will fall away or soften before it reaches you. It can even stop it altogether.

Robin and I have been friends since second grade. We consider each other family. I was the first to settle down, and Robin went out to see the world. A few years later, I received a letter from her, brimming with delight and details over meeting a man named John, her soul mate. Robin was coming home with her new husband.

I noticed that Robin was nervous when she introduced John and soon realized he was a man who said whatever came to mind. He got a big kick out of shocking people. I found it difficult to be around him. No matter how hard I tried to plan time with just Robin, John always found a way to be included.

Being at a loss for what do, I asked my Guardian Angel to stand in front of me whenever I was around John. Now, when he speaks with sarcasm or ignorance, his tone, mannerisms, intentions and words must first pass through pure Angelic energy before reaching my space. This eradicates or softens John's energy. By the time it truly reaches me, I can usually brush it away.

Interact With Other Beings Of Light
A new perspective ~ Wisdom from above
A clearing of thought and intention
Why didn't I think of that before?

Light Beings are great at finding the middle ground and the highest good for the circumstance. When you cannot reach a resolution face to face, consider looking to a Higher Source for assistance.

James and Alice married for all the right reasons. They loved and liked each other. They were also in love and respected each other. They shared common goals, morals and ethics, and intended to grow as individuals and as partners.

James loved football and fishing. After a long week at work, he looked forward to watching the game on Sunday. During the spring and summer, putting his boat in the water and spending the day fishing was probably the most relaxing thing he could do. It calmed his mind, restored his energy and made him happy.

Alice loved bookstores and renovating the house. A Saturday afternoon spent in a bookstore regenerated her energy. The visual beauty of the books, the written word, and the new information to be shared restored her sense of self after her own long week at work. It also gave her ideas for decorating and improving the house. Sunday was her chance to work on her home. She was adding her favorite colors, textures, and finishes to their house, one room at a time.

Meanwhile, you would find James watching football or fishing on Sunday. It was not long before they began to bicker. James wanted to relax, and Alice wanted his help. Soon James began to feel guilty about putting his feet up, while Alice struggled to paint a vaulted ceiling or replace a faucet. The discrepancy slowly became a source of cutting remarks that colored their relationship.

They tried to compromise and put these differences to rest. Unfortunately, they kept reverting to old habits and became more quarrelsome. He felt defensive, and she felt unheard. This issue was eroding their relationship.

It occurred to both of them, that they needed help to resolve their weekend bickering. James asked his Angel to talk to Alice's Angel. He just wanted Alice to understand that he needed some time to himself. The result was that Alice's Angel gave her a thought to consider in a manner that she would not feel pushed. Since it was her thought and not his words, she was open to seeing the issue through a new perspective. Then her Angel talked to James's Angel and did the same. Now, on Saturdays, they work on the house together. On Sundays, he watches the game or goes fishing, while she browses through the bookstore. This solution creates no guilt. Nothing is taken personally, and it meets the needs of both. They have both added wisdom and enlightenment to their lives and souls.

Give You A Break

Relax your shoulders and breathe
A gentle breeze of peace ~ Just be for now
All is well

Angels can give you a vacation from Earth School lessons until you are ready to move forward. It can be as short as recess, lunchtime, or as long as a year's sabbatical. Ask for a break when you feel the need to rest or re-group. Then, get back into the Classroom.

John's life lessons seemed to be coming too fast. He had lost his job that February and could not find new employment. Even the fast food restaurants were turning him away. Without a paycheck, he could only hold onto his house for a few more months. The kids needed money for school, and he felt terrible telling them he didn't have money to give. He was able to make a few dollars that spring picking up odd jobs, mostly moving furniture or mowing lawns. When he was beginning to get his feet under him, his car broke down, and the repair took the last of his savings.

He needed a break, so he asked for one. Reaching deep inside, he asked for aid, just a short time of peace, so he could lay down his problems.

That night the phone rang. John was pleasantly surprised to hear from an old friend he had not heard from in years. An hour of reminiscing was just what he needed to lay his burdens down and refocus on the good in life. It was the perfect vacation for the circumstance.

160

Other Angels

Our Guardian Angels are but one of a vast array of Angels on the Earth School Campus. Each of the many types of Angels is a unique blending of pure radiance that projects from the illumination of God. Just as souls have definition and shape, so do Angels. All Messengers of Grace manifest in a form that exemplifies their function. An Angel's appearance is a statement of purpose and intent. They are what they seem to be.

Angels of Protection exude strength and power. Many times they manifest wearing armor. Messenger Angels move quickly and present with streamlined forms for expediency. Cherubim appear childlike with wings just large enough to keep them aloft. They do not rush but hover to hold the space in Angelic Light. They manifest where they can be useful.

Angel's wings symbolize their effortless movement between all dimensions. With just a glance, each wing shape and size reveals what aspect of God's uniquely blended energy each angel represents. Huge, arched, powerful wings, feathered or smooth, angled or straight— they each help define the purpose of the Messengers of Hope. I have seen tiny wings on the back of large Angels, almost as if they were an afterthought. They were powerful Angels that stood their ground and held firm.

Wings are also a representation of the energy, skill and power of Light Beings of Grace. Some Angels have the wingspan of a golden eagle, and others resemble the wings of a hummingbird. No two are the same. Many wings are heavily feathered, with each feather lifting, moving and settling independently. This action causes the energy to flow just a little differently than when the feathers lay uniformly, creating a smooth surface.

Archangels

Archangels are strong powerful Beings of Light that extend from The Creator. I have personally seen four Archangels:

Archangel Michael

Michael is a vast Light Beam streaming from the Creator. This divine Archangel originates from the nucleus of God. He manifests wearing armor, ready for battle holding the Sword of Truth—a heavy polished blade in his right hand. When Michael slams the tip of the sword into the ground Light bounces off the sheen of the metal. Only truth can exist in the area of illumination once this is done. He is a warrior for protection against evil and darkness. This is the gift of Michael the Archangel—protection for our souls from all who would do us harm.

When you ask for his help, Archangel Michael is with you before your request is uttered. Without hesitation, he rises to your aid no matter what dimension, level or dilemma you are in.

Michael stands ready with his sword to serve all who call for his assistance. He uses The Sword of Truth to cut away that which is no longer needed in our lives by clearing obstacles, negativity, foreign energy or debris that can cling to or threaten us. This Angel is concerned with protecting all the parts of you as you go through your Classes. Michael brings you empowerment to help you be all that you are.

If you are facing a situation that seems impossible to resolve and is causing you stress and pain, call upon Michael to help you resolve issues, then act to become part of the solution.

Ms. Lucy is a woman of strong opinion and does not hesitate to express herself—loudly. She is a member of a small community who allows her to rein over the town with a strong hand.

The mayor's son, Jake, was planning his wedding and knew he was expected to invite Ms. Lucy. This was so distasteful to him that he came to me for help. Together, we asked for guidance from a higher source and were shown Archangel Michael. Having experience with Michael's help, I asked that he cast his Sword of Truth down the middle of the chapel on Jake's wedding day. Knowing that only Light and truth can exist around the radiance of the Sword, we also asked that it be present in the reception hall as well. Jake seemed pleased with this and soon the day of his wedding was here.

Ms. Lucy's car pulled up to the front of the church and her strong energy was immediately felt. It seemed as if a small tornado was swirling towards the chapel. However, that energy seemed to dissipate with each step that she took up the front steps. she seemed to become somewhat mellow. She and her husband chose a seat near the back door, where she remained quiet and respectful during the service.

Next, was the reception, and again, the space felt sacred, joy-filled and happy. Here comes Ms. Lucy, well known for taking over community events. Her antics on the dance floor usually got her all the attention in the room—and not in a good way.

She approached the wedding party and in a soft voice, congratulated the new couple, then found her table. When the dancing began, Ms. Lucy told her husband that her feet hurt, her shoes were too tight, and she didn't feel like dancing. She wanted to go home. And that is what she did. Ms. Lucy's usual energy was fast-paced, chaotic and irritating. She could easily overwhelm other people's energy. However, when her force encountered the Light energy of Archangel Michael, she felt the need to leave so she could return to her chosen frequency of commotion and erratic power. It was her choice.

Another way to work with the energy of Archangel Michael is to clear the clutter in your life. Do your part by clearing disorder from all the parts of you—mind, body and soul. Thank all these things for once having served you. Then, bless them, and ask Michael to carry their residual energy away to where they will do no harm.

I always ask Archangel Michael to place The Sword of Truth at the end of my driveway or my front door when people visit. In this way, any entities and negativity they have brought with them must wait for them outside. This leaves my house clean and clear.

Archangel Gabriel

Gabriel watches over all souls. She is the messenger of the mysteries of God, especially the many faces of The Creator and all the anonymities related to it.

Archangel Gabriel also inspires and motivates artists and communicators, helping them to overcome fear and procrastination. Gabriel is an Advocate for those who desire change and demonstrate a willingness to be helpful. Call upon Archangel Gabriel for guidance if you are an artist, author, musician, singer, songwriter, teacher, or if you do anything involving delivering spiritual messages. Gabriel will open doors to help you express your talent.

I am a great starter of projects and my garage is filled with boxes storing the ones I have abandoned for now. Many ideas that were planned, started but not finished are covered in layers of dust. They are things I plan to make time for someday, but not today and probably not tomorrow. It is sometimes easier to become distracted rather than finish what I start.

My problem is over thinking. I reason that before I can do a project, I should make that phone call first, and then I must run to the store. When I think about it, I get stuck. Being aware of this tendency in myself and fearing that procrastination could occur in completing, **Welcome to Earth School**, I asked Archangel Gabriel to help motivate me to finish it to the best of my ability. The advice I received from Gabriel is, "Don't think about it just do it." She also sent me Divine motivation. Now I can't put it down. I don't know how to write a book, publish or market, yet doors are opening, leading me in positive directions.

Gabriel has long been known as a powerful and strong Archangel. Those who call upon her will find themselves encouraged into action.

Archangel Raphael

Archangel Raphael's specialty is helping us open our hearts and souls to the healing power within ourselves. He assists us in being a catalyst for recovery. There is a saying on the Earth Campus, "God helps those who help themselves." in other words taking on the responsibility of using our talents and gifts in such a way that we have more abundance for ourselves. Raphael also brings to us the wisdom that whatever healing we are seeking. However, we must do our part by creating a channel through which the healing can flow.

Archangel Raphael is also a Champion of forgiveness. This does not involve accepting what was done to us, but rather by our refusing to carry such heaviness as anger, resentment and pain any longer. He also stands at the ready if you need help with the forgiveness process, especially when we find that sometimes the hardest person to forgive is ourselves.

United Flight 99 was boarding first class passengers and those that needed assistance. Our vacation was about to begin. I was assigned to the middle seat in a row that butted up to a dividing wall that left no extra room to navigate the narrow entrance into my row. There was a man already sitting in the aisle seat. I smiled and said, "Excuse me, but my seat is on the other side of you," hoping he would get up and allow me to get to my seat. He responded by glaring at me as I struggled to get past him. It only took a few seconds for me to realize that he did not believe in personal hygiene. When we reached altitude, he pulled out his lunch, which was a large sandwich stuffed with onions, garlic, peppers, oil and salami—the aroma was strong. Twice during the flight, I excused myself to use the restroom, but he refused to move at all. His feet remained planted in the narrow passage. Upon returning to my aisle, I asked him if he could move just a little, so I could get back in my seat. He growled and said, "Just get in."

When the plane landed at our destination and the aisles were emptying out, I said, "Okay, it's our turn." He looked at me and said, "I don't want to get off yet." Now I was mad. Instead of stepping over him, I purposely stepped on his feet, and ground my shoes on his as I stumbled over him. Storming into the terminal, I was so incredulous that I had to sit down in the waiting area. I was fuming, until I looked up and saw the man roll by me in his wheelchair. He was paralyzed from the waist down.

Right there in the terminal, I asked Archangel Raphael to help me understand what had just happened. My anger had been quick to rise up, and I had no problem assuming the worst about that man. On the other hand, he could have explained himself. Regardless, I wanted to forgive myself and the paralyzed man, let go of my anger and learn the lesson—you never know for sure what the other person's state of mind or circumstances may be.

Archangel Raphael reminds me not to give away my power by allowing frustration, judgment, and anger to grow larger than my compassion and patience.

Archangel Uriel

Archangel Uriel is associated with the unimaginable Light of God, which gives you illumination. When you ask for his help, he brings Divine Light into your life as he transforms painful memories and restores peace to your past.

This Archangel's purpose is to assist you in securing yourself in love that is strong enough to withstand any negativity. This powerful Archangel helps you turn your worst disappointments into your greatest blessings, while recognizing the teachings in your life.

Also, as the Archangel of Transformation, Uriel can show us how to heal every aspect of our lives, turning failures into victories, finding blessings in adversity, and releasing the painful burdens and memories of the past through unconditional forgiveness. Uriel uses Light to purify mental and emotional understanding and to transform lower vibrational energies into enlightened spiritual understanding. Archangel Uriel will assist you by inspiring brilliant new ideas to enter your mind.

The Archangel Uriel is traditionally also considered the Angel of the Earth. Therefore, Uriel is the patron of Ecology, the science of the whole Earth and the inter-relationship of all life upon it.

John Denver was a popular artist who was a talented troubadour and advocate for a healthy planet. One of his last concerts was in Southern Oregon, where his thousands of new friends warmly received his message of love and empowerment. When John died in a plane crash, a short time later, Archangel Uriel began to spread those spiritual messages in John's name, turning a painful ending into a call to continue his life's work.

All of the Archangels are steadfast Protectors and Champions of Peace.

Cherubim Angels

Cherubim represent all that is innocent, yet wise. They glow from the Heart of God. Usually gathered together, they float around your Being with their Light energy. If they perceive that you could use additional assistance, they will reach out to other Messengers of Grace to come to your aid.

Cherubim can share your laughter and tenderly catch your tears to comfort you. They help souls that have just arrived at Earth School to settle into their body by bridging the gap between the dimensions. People who have heard the resounding energy of a baby's laugh will understand the spirit of Cherubim.

When Aiden heard that his grandmother was ill, he called out to the Cherubim Angels. "Please bring laughter and glimmers of sunlight to my grandmother, who is going through a difficult time. Gather around her to provide support and companionship so that she will not feel alone. Bring forth the positive in her day and overwhelm the negative so that she can see clearly beyond this one moment in time to what is yet to be. Please lift my grandmother's spirit."

Seraphim Angels

Seraphim are swift Messengers for all Light Beings. They seek out helpful information and bring it where it might be useful. Their advice can reveal itself as a new thought, book, person or place that presents information to the inquiring soul. They can also carry a message from you to others in the Light.

Seraphim Angels will step forward to support you in what is useful and step back when you ask for what is useless. This is true of all Beings of Grace. They will not help you to be harmful or negative to yourself or anyone else, nor will they stop you from being foolish or unkind, as that would impede your free will. However, they will aid anyone who asks for their assistance in shielding, diverting or standing strong at their side. If the lesson is meant to be experienced, they will encourage you to use all the tools available to you. They will not remove the lesson, but will support you through it.

Ilene was visiting Ireland, when she began to think of Angels. She felt a strong need to connect to their Divinity, but was at a loss on what to do. She whispered a little request to her Guardian Angel, Bob, to help her find the information she was seeking. Bob in turn sent out an Angelic request to the Seraphim Angels to obtain answers and deliver them to him or directly to Ilene through Divine intervention.

While she was walking the streets of Kilkenny, a soft rain began to fall. Ilene ducked into the closest shop and found herself in a small bookstore. The shop was not just small but perhaps the size of a deep closet. She laughed, thinking it must have been built for leprechauns. With four people already packed into it, she found herself unable to move about. When the other patrons shifted their position in the shop, Ilene tried to step into another spot, but there was no room. Her foot kept tapping up against a pile of books on the floor. She looked down and saw, a stack of books, written by an Irish author, titled "Angels in My Hair." It had such a curious name that she could not look away. She felt compelled to buy it. Later that night, she discovered it contained the information she had been hoping for.

Herabim Angels

Herabim Angels step into seemingly overwhelming circumstances. They strive to shield the innocent. I would compare them to a special police unit, like the S.W.A.T. team. They surround you with Angelic Light. They can assist all your aspects—physical, emotional, mental and spiritual.

Herabim Angels can take many forms. Often, they will take the form of an animal, such as a horse, dog or cat. Tangible and solid, their physical presence can be the best way to help a soul. Some students on the Earth Campus cannot express what they are feeling. Autism, depression, and emotional or mental distress are a few of the causes. However, many times those students will respond to an animal with distinct Herabim energy. That energy is total acceptance, love and pure connection to Spirit.

Early one morning, I was woken by the phone ringing. The woman on the other end was distraught and asked for my assistance. She explained that she and her two young sons had just returned from a memorial for Henry and were grief-stricken. I had just begun to share my spiritual gifts and was not certain I could help her so I asked God: "Can I? May I? Should I?"

I received the answer "yes" for all three questions. Although I felt timid, I sensed the opportunity to help people who were suffering. I needed to put my shyness aside.

I asked her not to tell me anymore about the situation and to please call me back in two hours when I would have uninterrupted time. I find it easier to access my energetic gifts when I have no preconceived ideas or information. It allows my mind to be silent and my soul to be fully in the moment.

When she called back, the only thing I saw with my clairvoyance was a big cat that walked past me. Thinking it was a distraction, I dismissed the cat and tried to clear my mind and focus from my soul. Again, the cat walked past me. This continued to happen until I asked to be shown Henry. The big cat walked up to me, nose to nose.

At a loss about what to do, I finally told the woman I could not help her. I was not being shown anything. As an afterthought, I casually mentioned that a big cat kept looking at me, at which time the woman exclaimed, "Henry!" Then her story began to unfold before me.

Their family had been in turmoil for the past few years. The father had become abusive and unleashed his rage on his wife and two small sons. When it began, a stray kitten wandered out of the forest and into their home. The boys had named him Henry. He settled into the family and simply came into the room and held the space when the father's negativity swirled in and out of the house. The cat was silently buffering the height of the rage from the innocent family members.

Eventually, the father left and the turmoil no longer existed. The cat stayed for a time to comfort the family and smooth the erratic energy that remained. A few months later, Henry walked back into the woods and was not seen again. The mother and her two sons held a memorial for him the day of our phone call.

I was able to tell the woman about Herabim Angels and how they often took the form of an animal to help people through challenging times. I saw that Henry had been such an Angel. Now, they knew that an Angel had been part of their family to assist them through a difficult time in their lives. This knowledge comforted them and helped them face their loss as well.

Henry was yet another Herabim Angel who saw a need, took the form of a comforting presence, and stepped in to help.

Herabim can also lift a soul out of its human body before it experiences what seems to be a painful event. Here is an example:

A dear friend asked me to meet with a woman named, Marie, who had recently lost her teen-age daughter, Sophia, in an auto accident. Marie was uncertain of what I might offer her, but agreed to meet anyway.

Instead of meeting at my home, we met at Sophia's resting place. I arrived early, and within minutes, Sophia appeared to me in spirit form, gracefully dancing around the edges of her grave and tenderly touching the items her friends had left for her—wind chimes, flowers, pictures and teddy bears. I asked Sophia to share with me how she had crossed over.

Part of my job is to stay clear from another's energy, so that soul energies are not co-mingled. This allows me to remain whole and clear, but in this instance, I allowed Sophia to show me, through her eyes, the events she experienced.

She and I, from one joined viewpoint, were in a small truck. I could see a turn in the road up ahead and also sensed a male sitting next to us. As we came to the turn, the truck seemed to melt away, and we were flying, arms extended, head lifted, laughing and twirling as we rose higher and higher. We looked like Wendy in Peter Pan.

Herabim Angels had lifted her soul out of her body just before the curve in the road. I heard her maternal grandmother, who was on the other side laughing in delight, as we soared up to her arms. Sophia's life plan did not include crossing in fear, nor was it in her highest good, so she received aid from Herabim Angels. That is exactly how Sophia's time in Earth School ended.

When Marie arrived at the cemetery for our meeting, she appeared to be suffering greatly. As Sophia lightly stepped to her mother's side and rested her head on her shoulder, she told me what her mother had experienced on the day of the accident.

A California Highway Patrol car had pulled into their driveway, and an officer told Marie that her daughter had been in a terrible accident. He surmised that Sophia had missed a sharp curve in the road. As her truck left the pavement, it flipped several times. She was thrown from the truck and crushed under the vehicle. They found no way to save her.

When Marie found out that Sophia was gone, her grief was so strong that her Guardian Angel, Celestine, immediately surrounded her with violet Light. Violet is the strong, direct Light of the Creator, the same place Sophia's astral soul had just entered. Marie did not feel so disconnected from her daughter, because she was also surrounded by God's Light.

Celestine helped buffer the deep cut of extreme grief and held her through all the stages of her anguish. The Angel kept watch over her soul Light, feeding it slowly with healing energy. Marie's ocean of tears would all but wash it away and again Celestine would tend to her, gently breathing Light into the darkest parts of her day. The Angel stood guard, helping Marie manage her pain and prevent it from becoming so unstable as to harm other parts of her.

Celestine encouraged Marie to find balance and sustain her physical body with rest and food. She wrapped peaceful energy around Marie when she was exhausted and when her emotions fluctuated between despair and the surging rush of anger. Celestine also called upon the Angels of Healing for extra assistance. Together, they helped Marie to walk through this difficult journey.

There had been a passenger in the truck with Sophia that day, who was bruised, but otherwise unharmed. Everyone said it was a miracle that he was not badly injured. He came away from the accident very confused as to what he had witnessed. Sophia had been chatting with him when the accident happened. He told Marie, "Sophia had no reaction at all. She continued to steer straight ahead instead of turning with the curve. Her smile never left her face, no panic, just calmness." He repeatedly told the story, trying to make sense of it. As the messenger for Sophia, I told Marie all I was shown and emphasized that her daughter had experienced no pain. Sophia's Higher Self had planned to attend Earth School for sixteen years and then to continue her soul journey in a different way. Sophia's soul energy came from the heart of The Highest Light and was from the energetic group, The Children of God. They usually cross over at a young age because their energy is simple joy. It is too tenderhearted to remain on the Earth Campus into adulthood.

Children of God are a gift to all of us. When a young person crosses over, the entire community pays attention and is reminded of the value of time and the importance of love. Sophia told her mother many things that were happening for her sisters since she had left the Earth Campus, as confirmation to Marie that her daughter was speaking to her.

Marie left the cemetery still in grief, but she had hope in her eyes. Her heart was open to receiving Sophia's continuing love and she held a deeper knowing that her daughter continued on.

Please keep in mind that some people in accidents do experience the entire event, if it is meant to be for a learning purpose as one of the last lessons they experience in Earth School. However, many people cross over without feeling all that is happening to their physical body.

Guardian Angels, Archangels, Heraphim, Seraphim or Cherubim—Angels are the magnificent Light Beams of God that will shine with you for eternity.

Gifts and Tools

You have all that you need

to become an accomplished soul

Gifts are meant to enhance and help us on our Earth School journey through our Classes and lessons. When we ignore our unique mental, emotional, spiritual or physical talents, our gifts remain unopened or disregarded. If we decide to express or bring forth harmful energy, it is a skill misused. The possibilities of a richer life journey increase tenfold when you use all of your talents and abilities in a positive manner.

For example, you may have the ability to make sense of complicated issues, to foresee what is possible or to comfort others in their time of need. You could have a talent for deep spirituality, peace or calmness. There is no limit to the number of gifts souls are given.

While you attend Earth School, you are a soul that has experiences within a human body. Some Students fail to remember that, and believe they are a human being who has occasional spiritual encounters. Utilizing your gifts as you move through your School courses will provide you with more information and the possibility of increased wisdom.

You also have more tools to enhance the experience of your environment than your physical senses of hearing, sight, touch, taste and smell. Many of you have discovered that you are multisensory and have energetic and spiritual skills that take you beyond this three-dimensional reality.

Using both your spiritual abilities and the talents of your physical senses can provide you with added tools to enrich your opportunities to learn and grow while you attend Earth School Classes. What are these abilities?

- Clairvoyance: Seeing with your inner vision what cannot be seen with your physical eyes

- Clairaudience: Hearing within your soul without the use of physical ears

- Clairalience: Distinct energetic smelling without the use of the nose and where there is no physical source of scent

- Clairgustance: The pure taste of spirit, tasting what is not visible or physical

- Clairsentience: Feeling with your spirit, sensing with you soul.

- Telepathy: Communicating with thought without the use of words or signs

- Intuition: Knowing in your very Being what is not evident

When you are aware of and use these talents of soul-body connection, you navigate through your life journey and Earth School lessons with a greater understanding of the larger picture. These skills connect you to what is not immediately apparent in the physical sense, yet still exists. Your passions will help you identify your talents—mental, physical, emotional, spiritual, multisensory and energetic.

For those Students who struggle to find theirs, here are suggestions:

- Pay attention to what your life shows you.
- If you had to speak for one hour to hundreds of people, what topic would you choose to speak about?
- What subjects fully engage you?
- In what areas are you most effective?

There are usually three steps involved in growing into your best self:

FIND your gift within yourself.

DEFINE every aspect of it.

REFINE your gifts and blend them into your life and soul journey

Find your gifts. If you have difficulty identifying them, ask trusted friends what they see in you. Ask yourself these questions: Have you ever known what was going to happen just before it occurred? Have you ever known the phone was going to ring, and it did? Have you ever thought of another person, and that person called? Do you have a gut reaction to the energy that surrounds you? What do you see when your eyes are closed? Do you hear sounds, words or music inside of yourself? Can you smell something that is not present? Do you experience a taste when nothing is held in your mouth? Would you rather document the moment, speak about it or help others through it? Do you have a strong sense of order and organization? Are you gifted in listening, observing or seeing complicated situations with clarity? Are you passionate about protecting the innocent or healing the injured? Are you a champion for animals? What would you like to change about mankind? What part of you connects to something greater than yourself? What do you know on a soul level?

Define your gifts. Explore the avenues and paths that mean the most to you. What would you like to do with your abilities? Ask for help in improving your talents on the physical plane as well as on the spiritual.

Refine your gifts. Become practiced in your area of expertise. This will lead you to become empowered, confident and living a life of purpose.

You can define your talents and refine what you are willing to offer others through those talents. The phases of this process can overlap each other and change as your Earth School Classes and lessons change.

Remember, each talent is unique unto itself. When you pay attention to your skills and use them well, you will feel more passionate, motivated, successful and complete. Use these feelings as guidelines. When they are present, they show you that you are following the right direction for the growth of your soul.

An example of a physical gift is having the ability to be a great football player. However, if you never pick up a football, practice and have coaches help you refine your ability, it will remain a talent that is not fully developed. As a result, you do not grow as a football player. Ignoring your spiritual gifts and their development impedes the growth of your soul.

Consider sharing your talents with others that ask. As with any aptitude, you can use it with positive intent, negative intent or anything in between. You might choose to ignore it, deny it, or be lazy with it, or afraid of it. Or, you can decide to be grateful for it, practice it, perfect it and use it with enthusiasm. You decide what to do with your energetic abilities. Knowing they exist will give you more insight into your true self—the whole of your soul, unencumbered by foreign energy and free of outside input, persuasion or interference.

The process is not unlike examining a flower. Each blossom is unique and each petal is layered around the center, creating a complete object capable of stimulating many of your senses. It has color, aroma, form, texture and visual appeal. The purpose of a flower is to be a flower. Your purpose is to be you, with all of your layers forming one complete Being in harmony with yourself.

Our spiritual gifts are the ones people seem to have the greatest challenge identifying, developing and refining. They are not visible to the human eye, but held in our soul energy. Many people do not believe or give attention to what is not easily seen, touched or known to them.

We are going to focus on these abilities of spirit, because we were given them for a reason—to help guide us through our soul journey and evolution and to connect to something greater than ourselves.

The Gift of Clairvoyance
Clair meaning clear—Voyance meaning sight

To be clairvoyant is to see without your physical eyes. This is the ability to see more than what is clear in the third dimension. Many of us on the Earth Campus are aware that we live in a place where not all that exists can be seen with our physical eyes. Air currents, creative energy, love and anger are energies not visible with the eyes of the body, yet they are present just the same. Knowing this gift exists is important, as well as understanding how to use it for your highest good.

When people with the gift of clairvoyance close their eyes, they might see colors, pictures, words, faces, just about anything. Many can see with both their inner and outer vision simultaneously. The questions they might ask would be—What does it mean? Where is the image coming from? Why am I seeing it and what can I learn from it?

When students on the Earth Campus sit down to watch television, they first plug the cord into an energy outlet, and then tune it to the channel of their choosing. They might decide to watch a game show, The Learning Channel or the local news. There are programs for just about any age and taste.

If you have the gift of clairvoyance, you can learn to view different sources, just as you do with a television. Will you watch energy from the highest realm, the in-between levels, or the darkest space? Consider viewing what is valuable and dismiss or block what is not.

Here is a look at how to tell the difference: Picture this—you live in a little house and are quite comfortable. One morning, you wake up to find a television in your living room. You feel somewhat unsettled, because you do not know how it got there. You have heard about televisions, but since you have never had one before, you are not sure how to operate it.

As the day continues, the television suddenly goes on by itself and is tuned to the news. All day long, the TV goes on and off without you doing anything and changes to random channels. It frightens you. What first looked like a gift has turned into a nuisance.

The next morning you wake up to find televisions in every room. You have no control over which ones are on, which ones are off, or what stations they play. Living with the televisions feels chaotic and overwhelming.

Just as you would not allow an unknown source to place televisions in your house, do not allow your inner vision to be bothered by useless visual pictures. Using your free will, you have the right to decide what you are willing to view and when.

Consider another option: What if a trusted teacher asked your permission to place one or more televisions in your house? Then the teacher gave you the remote control, taught you how to use it, and suggested which stations you might find interesting and valuable. As you gained experience, you learned which channels attracted you and which ones filled your home with negativity. You have now gained control of this gift.

Beginning to see with your inner vision can be as much a surprise as an unexpected television.

Think about your own life for a moment. Is it not true that many things worth having began with some fear? In learning to walk, we overcome our fear of falling. In opening our heart to love, we risk being hurt. In being our true self, we run the chance of being ridiculed by those who do not understand.

The soul is resilient. What is wounded can heal. When we fall, we get back up and try again. When we love with every fiber of our Being, we are courageous and brave.

Will you shut out what is visible with the eyes of your soul, because you might see something unpleasant or misleading? Or, will you choose to stand strong and see what is decent, Light and helpful?

I have witnessed people shut their physical eyes in fear for a moment, but I have yet to meet someone who refuses to open their eyes preferring to be blind. Instead, people have learned to look away and monitor what they are willing to view when the sight in front of them brings up discomfort. But if they decide to look at what is potentially harmful, they can choose to deal with it head on, perceive it with clarity and take the necessary steps to stop it if need be. Should you not do the same with your inner vision as you do with your outer one?

Just as you decide what to look at in your life, you can also choose what to look at with your inner vision. Learn to filter out the unnecessary trash using your mind-body-soul connection. When you make the choice to open up all of your vision, both the outer and inner sight, you can see what is immediately in front of you and what is visible with the eyes of your soul. Then, you get to decide what merits your attention. I encourage you to practice standing strong and using your powerful energy to dismiss the negative and invite the positive.

Placing strong safeguards around you helps to keep intruders at bay. If they still break through your protection, learn about more tools with which to shield yourself. We will cover how to protect yourself later in this chapter.

I spent my first eighteen years in Earth School understanding just the basics of what was best for me on the Campus, what was harmful and what was helpful to me.

As the years progressed, so did my comprehension of the world. They are called baby steps for a reason. You start as an infant and step-by-step, learn what works and what does not. As you move forward, you discover where you belong and where you do not, when to be quiet and when to be heard, what leads to trouble and what leads to wisdom.

Now, it was important to protect my emotions, mental state and soul Light in the same way that I guarded my physical aspect. This protection had to be strong, effective and courageous.

I learned to draw the line when evil approached on any level. I was not willing to be distracted by an unkind word, a lie told behind my back or by having my spirituality attacked. I drew boundaries on all levels and did my best to stop those who would inappropriately step over them.

I discovered that the energy of people, places and things had the potential to color my energy. However, I had the ability to decide what to allow in my home, in my life and around my soul. My intention became to participate in what improved all the parts of me by adding stronger positive energy. My intention was to become an enlightened soul.

The opportunities to learn come daily and never stop. All I have to do is pay attention to the moment, decide what to do with it, and move forward.

I have learned how important breath is. Just to breathe. It oxygenates the body, comforts the soul, calms emotion and energizes my mind. Breath brings all my parts together in the present moment.

Perhaps, the best of both physical and spiritual gifts of sight comes when you grow into a place of wisdom and understanding. Then, you know that no matter what you see, you are capable and willing to deal with it in a positive manner and step into the next moment.

The Gift of Clairaudience

Clair meaning clear — audience meaning sound

Clairaudience is the ability to hear without your physical ears. With this gift, you hear words, music, thoughts or sounds inside you. Learn to recognize your inner voice, the voice of God, and the voices of Light and Grace. Become skilled at recognizing the voice of negativity and how to silence it.

The gift of clairaudience is often misunderstood. Over the centuries, millions of students have been diagnosed with mental disorders, when in fact, many were hearing voices because they were clairaudient. Souls that dwell in the shadows were bothering them.

When you quiet the noise in your head, you can hear your soul—an accomplishment that can take practice, but is well worth the effort.

At times, clairaudient people will have a thought, which begins in their mind and suggests they are inadequate. Will you give credence to that thought by accepting it or recognize it for what it truly is—intrusive negative noise?

Hearing negative thoughts gives you the opportunity to learn how to silence them. State firmly:

"These are not my intended thoughts."

Insist they leave your presence and go back to where they came from—senseless negative space. That is where they originated, and that is where they belong. No one in the Light would cause you fear or frightening thoughts.

Become practiced at recognizing negative thoughts and outside voices. That is why the opportunities to hone and practice your ability to eliminate these thoughts and voices occur so often.

You can compare it to your physical world. Here, you learn to tune out the voices you find disruptive. You decide which sounds to pay attention to and which ones to ignore, which lessons to participate in and what Classes you will join. Would you willingly stand in front of a ranting person, who is spewing angry, irate words at you or listen to loud noise you find unsettling? Most students on a positive path will naturally gravitate toward voices and sounds that are pleasant and helpful to them.

If a person walks up to you and begins to shout obscenities or vulgar words, do you stay or walk away, knowing those words and thoughts have nothing to do with you? If an intruder is discovered in your home would you allow him to stay or send him on his way? You would ask, "Who are you and how did you get in here?" You might ask a friend to help eject him or call 911 for experienced support. Most likely, you would not stop until the person was gone.

And so it should be with your clairaudient ability. Be vigorous and steadfast in your determination to rid yourself of any thought, word or sound heard within yourself that is not in your highest good. When you dispose of the negative, you open up room for the positive.

Kristina wakes up almost every morning with a song playing inside of her head. Many times, that music brings to her mind lyrics of the song that carry a message of guidance for her that day.

How does she tell the difference between musical guidance from the Light or an interruption from the shadows? She asks the source of the song, "Are you in the Light? If not, then you must go." If the music continues, she knows the advice comes from the Light. If the song stops, even for a second, she has confirmed it comes from shadow.

Listen to guidance from Divine Grace, consider the words of your Angel and be comforted by encouraging music. Hear those in the Light, and move through your life journey with assurance and enlightenment. Be grateful for a splendid talent that brings you information and wisdom for yourself and to share with others.

The Gift of Clairalience
Clair meaning clear—alience meaning smell

Clairalience is the ability to clearly smell what exists on the energetic dimensions and is not present in the third dimension, the dimension of physical presence. This gift can be quite surprising and usually causes people to investigate physical sources for the scent, only to find none. Smell is simply another way we can receive information from other dimensions and from the energy of spirit.

A human being's sense of smell is the strongest memory trigger. The fragrance of a grandmother's perfume, the pungent aroma of an uncle's cigar smoke and the smells of childhood are deeply ingrained in the brain's memory. Aromas can create many emotions—pleasant sensations, emotional distress or comfort, or activate a remembrance of a time that has passed.

As people milled about after his grandfather's funeral service, Bob continued to sit on the hard wooden bench in the church. He wasn't yet ready to face anyone.

A sense of spirituality was not part of Bob's vocabulary. He believed that when you die, you are gone, forever. And now, his grandfather was gone, forever. No matter which way his mind turned, he ran into painful thoughts. He cried harder than he had ever cried before and still, the grief didn't budge. Eventually, he made his way home, dumped his suit on the floor, and wondered what to do next. Feeling restless, he aimlessly wandered around the house.

Something began to catch his attention—a smell that was somehow familiar, yet not associated with his home. As he followed it toward the back of the house, the scent became stronger. The sweet smell of leather and vanilla tobacco, which he associated with his grandfather, was swirling around Bob's back room. In that moment, without a doubt or reservation, Bob knew his grandfather was there with him, to calm him, to assure him that life went on, and to let him know that he was thriving. He felt so much comfort from those scents. That day a seed of contentment was planted in Bob's soul, and in an instant, his view of life and what happens in the afterlife changed.

Clairalience is a form of extrasensory perception that gives a person access to spiritual knowledge through the physical sense of smell.

The Gift of Clairgustance
Clair meaning clear—gustance meaning taste

The gift of clairgustance is the talent that allows individuals to taste a substance without putting anything on their tongue. Instead, they perceive the essence of energy of that substance from the spiritual or ethereal realms using their ability of clairgustance.

Lisa is a psychologist who is employed at a law corporation as a specialist in juror selection. She is highly recognized and paid for her ability to discern personality types or the energy that people project. When she came to see me I was shown that she has a remarkable skill of clairgustance. She possessed the ability to literally taste the energy present in a person.

Being in the presence of manipulators and liars left a bad taste in her mouth and dried her tongue. As soon as she could, Lisa would scramble to down a cool glass of water to clear the taste from her mouth.

For Lisa, infants had a lingering fresh flavor, like a clean breeze swirling around her. A zesty tang of exuberance accompanied the presence of friends. Positive energy was light and tasted clean. Negative energy caused her tongue to feel thick and foreign. When she paid attention, Lisa had more information about people and her environment than many other individuals.

However, Lisa was not consciously aware that she had any special talent in this area. She believed everyone could have the same experiences she did—all they had to do was pay attention. Until we spoke, she had not identified her ability as a gift of spiritual discernment.

Now that she knows clairgustance is a gift, she practices gratitude for it and uses it with the intention that it be for the betterment of all. Lisa also uses her tools to clear her palate of any outside energy, so it doesn't become part of her. To do this, she takes a deep breath and exhales with the intention of cleansing her energy.

Have you ever watched talented wine tasters? With a small sample of wine, they can connect the grapes to their place of origin, the year they were planted, the smooth sweetness or grainy rich structure. One swig of wine offers them a wealth of information.

Flavor can also stimulate a memory of experiences that also involve the senses of smell, taste, touch and sight. The physical taste of brown sugar can bring remembrances of childhood holidays past baking in the family kitchen. It can bring to mind people, places and things of sentiment. Those with the gift of clairgustance have the chance to savor their life journey in a unique manner.

Telepathy

To communicate directly from one person's mind to another's without using speech, writing, or other signs or symbols, reveals telepathic ability. How often do people communicate so thoroughly that no one is confused by the other's meaning or intent? Frequently, words can be misunderstood or misused. With telepathic communication, the message or sharing of thoughts is clean, pure and simple.

Two people with telepathic abilities can be silent and still pick up one another's thoughts. However, those individuals can also experience times when one or both of them are distracted, not present in the moment or open to receive each other's thoughts as clearly.

My sister Mary lived on the east coast and I lived in the west. All I had to do was think about her and she would call. You will probably have that experience many times in your life. You might have a passing thought of someone. Soon, they will call and the conversation will start with the words, "I was just thinking about you."

Consider the thought you created as energy sent to that person. They receive that flow of energy, most often not being conscious that they are doing so, and choose to either respond or put it aside. Telepathic communication is not random or coincidental, but energy sent with intent.

Clairsentient Gift
Clair meaning clear—sentient meaning to sense

The clairsentient gift gives you the ability to feel what is not tangible in the physical world. You will be able to sense it in your soul and body. This ability will give you a gut knowing of the energy present.

Clairsentient people who do not yet understand this ability and how to manage it, tend to have stomachaches or digestive problems. This gift is held in the solar plexus area of the body. Some cultures refer to it as your third chakra, which is found about five inches above your navel. Having this gut response can serve as a signal that something is wrong—pay attention. At its best, the clairsentient skill gives you the talent to discern the energy around you and enhances your School experience.

This talent can be even stronger when you do not allow foreign energy into that area of your body. Foreign energy is all energy that is not purely your own. Students on the Earth Campus tend to allow other people's opinions, judgments and criticisms to invade this area of self. This can cloud their clarity. Detect the presence of outside energetic energy at an arm's length, before it can intertwine with your life force.

Clairsentient students usually flourish when they learn to live from their soul, not influenced by external energy. Live from your soul by consciously using your mind and emotions as sources of information, but using your soul for direction and decision. This gift will help you recognize the presence of negativity and the company of positive energy. The feeling can range from a sense of discomfort to an awareness of calmness, feelings of pure bliss or a mixture of emotions.

Learn to realize when impostors—other people, fearful feelings or thoughts, distractions or illusions—are misleading you, and put a stop to them. Become skilled at recognizing when you are in either a toxic situation or a circumstance that is healthy by paying attention to your senses.

Many people keep silent or do not take action when their clairsentient ability knows that something is not quite right about a person or a situation. Perhaps they do not want to appear impolite or are afraid of being told they are wrong.

If you have this ability, you can walk into a room and sense the energy in it. This talent gives you insight into what other people are energetically creating, releasing or holding. Being on the Earth Campus will help you understand this gift and hone your talent.

However, when you shut off your natural, instinctive gift, you deny what you know on a gut level. In the process, you open yourself to situations that could potentially harm you.

Clairsentience offers you chances to learn complicated lessons, such as how to recognize when you are safe or in physical danger. You can learn to distinguish the truth from a lie, when to move forward, hesitate, stop or turn around and go down a different path.

As a child with this ability, you will learn to size up situations. This goes beyond the elementary teachings from our parents, such as when something is hot, don't touch it or it will burn you. Or, don't run with sharp objects, you might fall and hurt yourself.

Far too many children are taught to ignore their clairsentient feelings. In fact, most little ones have this ability and learn to shut it off. Some adults believe this talent is socially unacceptable, or they do not understand being able to *feel* energy outside of themselves. A child might cry out to a parent, "Someone is in my closet, something is under my bed." They are sensing energy that feels uncomfortable to them. They may be too young to verbalize the feeling, but are never too young to sense it.

This true story explains the benefit of having the gifts of clairsentience and clairvoyance and what can happen when those around you understand it and help you to manage it.

Emma is thirty-two years old and lives in northern Michigan. When she was only five, her parents purchased an old Victorian house on the edge of their town. The house was run down and they planned to restore it to its original glory.

As a child, Emma was frightened in that house. She got to the point where she would not stay in a room by herself because she was too afraid. She missed quite a bit of school, because her stomach often hurt. Her parents tried doctors and changed her diet, hoping she would feel better, but nothing helped. Emma was shy and small, but most of all she was scared of the feelings inside of her. She did not have the vocabulary to explain to her parents that she felt heavy and sad energy in the living room. She could sense someone lingering in her bedroom, and she found it hard to breathe freely in the dining room.

Still, she tried the best she could to explain what was happening. Most parents under those circumstances would have opened all the cupboards and closets and looked under all the furniture to show Emma no one was there. Fortunately, Emma's parents believed her fear was based on something real and told her, "We love you. We believe you. Let's go find some help."

They brought her to see me. While Emma's mother settled in on the couch, I pulled out a basket of toys and played with her on the floor. Emma's Guardian Angel appeared to me. I told Emma, "You have the cutest little Angel. She reminds me of a fairy." Emma replied, "Yes, I know. She has her pink dress on today." She was right.

Emma was clairvoyant. She called Angels, fairies, and she had many around her. They thanked her for the house she had built for them in the tree behind her house. Using bark, ferns, stones and flowers, she had created a lovely woodland cottage in which they could flit about.

Now that we had gotten to know each other, it was important to empower Emma in what I perceived as her additional gift of clairsentience.

I explained that this was her time to be here, in the present, living her life. Her soul had come here to learn and grow. No one or nothing on any other dimension had the right to take that away from her by leaving or putting their energy into Emma's space. When a soul leaves the Earth Campus, it is not in anyone's highest good to leave behind their emotions such as fear, sorrow or negativity.

The Angels symbolically placed wide cuffs of silver around Emma's wrists and told her they were her tool to claim what was rightfully hers—this dimension and time. They were a symbol of power and strength. Emma said having the cuffs made her feel like a super hero.

I was shown that in the early 1900's, a family had lived in the same house Emma and her parents now owned. They had lived in chaos, distress and worry, and that energy was still present in the house. Those past energies were what Emma had been sensing. As we asked for help from the Highest Light, the angels responded. They flew in to the house and began to clean vigorously. They scrubbed the walls and doorframes, the floors and every speck of energy held in and on the house.

Emma and I watched it together. She was delighted. Her parents called me the next day to tell me that when they got home, Emma marched into each room, threw her arms in the air and announced, "Nobody belongs here, except me and my Angel." Almost immediately, Emma felt comfortable in all the rooms by herself. She had learned to acknowledge her feelings and to use her gifts and tools to clear her space.

Several months later, the family traveled to the local mall to buy a birthday present. Emma was tired of shopping and did not want to go into the candle store with her mom. She convinced her mother to allow her to sit on the bench just outside the doorway. Since her mother could keep an eye on her, she agreed.

Emma was enjoying watching all the different people walk by, until one man sat down next to her and began to speak to her. Immediately, her stomach got that feeling that something was wrong. His energy felt heavy and dark. Because her parents had confirmed her feelings months before, and had taken steps to teach her what to do, little Emma stood up and in her loudest voice yelled, "No one belongs here, except me and my Angel!"

As Emma's mother came rushing out of the store, the man hurried away. The fact that he ran gave Emma and her mother some confirmation of his intent.

Emma grew up. At age twenty, she became engaged to Jim. They had known each other since seventh grade and had dated through high school and college. Their family and friends expected them to get married.

However, Emma felt that old impression that something was wrong. She examined her feelings. She knew she loved Jim, but there were times he was moody or angry. Emma feared how far his temper would take him. Her stomach bothered her when she thought of a lifetime spent with him.

Regardless of what her family and friends were telling her, she paid attention to the red flags she sensed with her clairsentient gift. It told her that love was not enough to commit to a lifelong marriage with Jim.

While telling Jim that she could not marry him was extremely hard, she decided to go through those moments of stress and sadness rather than endure years of possible pain and a potentially dangerous situation. Jim did not take her decision well and pounded his fist through the wall. That verified to her that she had made the right decision.

Emma has learned to protect herself in all aspects of her life with her clairsentient skill—physically, emotionally, mentally and spiritually. Her talent alerts her to the energy present, giving her the opportunity to use her tools of protection to shield any part of her that might benefit from extra defense. Emma knows that when you ignore your instincts, you are dismissing your internal guidance. She calls it her feeling gift. This ability will serve her well for the rest of her life.

As you can see, every gift has many facets. The purpose is to learn from every angle how to apply your gift in your daily life.

The Gift of Intuition—Claircognizance

Intuition is the knowing of something you can only sense. This is the ability to recognize something without a physical explanation or intrinsic knowledge—a gift of realization on a soul level. Some people call this *spiritual knowing.*

If you are in an uncomfortable situation, and ignore your intuitive prompting to leave that situation, you could be setting yourself up for discomfort or anguish, until you listen to your wisdom of insight.

Still, Students often dismiss their intuition and allow their minds to point the way. Will you pay attention to what you know intuitively, and take the sometimes harder road that is in your highest good, or will you remain silent and ignore the action you're prompted to take? You always have a choice to use your gifts or ignore them.

The biggest rival of intuition is fear. The two can be easily confused. In a moment of uncertainty, how can you recognize the difference? How will you know if you are experiencing your talent of intuition or the emotion of fear?

Intuition is a gift of knowing held in your soul, while fear comes from the mind. It is good to experience both. That way, you can learn to recognize the difference and decide how to deal with any circumstance, either from a place of panic or using good judgment.

As soon as you feel something is wrong, pay attention. If the feeling comes from your head, fear is usually the cause. Clear your mind and breathe to be present in reality.

Sensing from your soul is intuition. Focus on what your intuition tells you.

Use your mind to think,
your heart to feel
and then decide with your soul.

When you ignore a warning it can come around a second time, only this time it can feel larger and perhaps more uncomfortable. The warning signals usually continue to increase the third time they appear, and so on. When you do not pay attention to your talent of intuition, you might generate unnecessary wounds by stepping onto the path you intrinsically know is not in your best interest. Accept your gift or live in fear of it. It is your decision. Remember, your intuitive knowing comes from your soul. Here is one circumstance that describes this ability, and how it can work.

Jared was on his way to Hawaii to surf off the north shore of the big island. He had dreamt of doing this since he was a child. After surfing for seven years off the coast of California, he felt ready for larger waves.

However, for some reason he could not quite explain, he felt a little nervous, and his stomach felt tight. He still had three hours before his plane landed, so he decided to nap, hoping to feel better when he woke up—he did not. That night at his hotel, his hands felt a little damp and shaky, so he turned in early.

The next morning as the sun came up over the horizon, Jared was not quite as eager to head for the ocean as he thought he would be. But he could find no logical reasons for his feeling, so he dismissed it. He walked out through the lobby and onto the beach. The clear seamless waves seemed perfect. Several surfers were already in the water. But, instead of joining them, he sat on the sand and watched for a while.

Jarod kept sensing an urge to flee and do something else. He tried to make sense of what seemed like an irrational feeling. Deciding he was not going to let fear stop him now, Jared finally waded into the warm water and easily paddled out beyond the break line to catch his first wave. He had no difficulty riding it all the way in. The rest of the morning was spent on the water, but the feeling that something was wrong continued to strengthen within him.

By early afternoon, he was sitting just beyond the break line, drifting in the breeze. Once again, he began to dig deep in the water with his cupped hands to catch the next wave that was already developing into a tube of liquid and foam. Before he knew it, he was shooting out of the pipeline, reaching high on the crest, and then scooting down to settle into the tunnel of water. Just as he was relaxing into the ride, the swift-moving water pulled his board from under his feet and at the same time, shoved him hard, straight down towards the bottom. He fought to push back to the surface, but could not tell which way was up.

The next moment, as he began to tumble in slow motion, was surreal. He was slammed onto the bottom of the ocean, and the impact forced out the little air he had left in his lungs. He lost consciousness. The last thing he remembered was the sound of roaring water and a loud crack from inside his body. He felt it as much as he heard it.

Several people on the beach watched with concern as Jared was thrown from his board and disappeared behind the wave. Two of them ran into the water in hopes of finding him.

Jared was lucky that day because people who knew what to do were able to save his life. He woke up in the hospital with a broken collarbone and three cracked ribs.

Jared's lesson in what can happen when you ignore your intuition was painful. But he also had a chance to learn, so that he could make a choice to follow promptings by his intuition in the future. Every time your gift makes itself known, and each time you follow or ignore it, you, like Jared, can learn valuable lessons in trusting what you know versus discovering what you are afraid of. Following your intuition means living from your soul.

Frequently, people wake up in the middle of the night knowing something has happened to a loved one. This is their intuitive talent working in conjunction with their soul, even as they sleep. Here are more cases of intuition from Student's lives.

~

Joe woke up in a cold sweat, with a heavy feeling in the pit of his stomach. He immediately knew that something was wrong with his son, Chris. A few minutes later, the phone rang with news that Chris had been in a car accident.

~

Every time I was around her, I got a red flag feeling a deep knowing that I should not trust her. Although I did not know it then, later I learned she was spreading falsehoods about me to my family and friends. I knew with my intuition that something was off and kept her at arm's length.

~

Kelei had decided to go back to work and began to interview potential nannies for her three-month-old son. Sara stood out from the rest with an impressive resume, but Kelei's intuition told her something wasn't quite right. She paid attention and may have possibly avoided an abusive situation for her little boy.

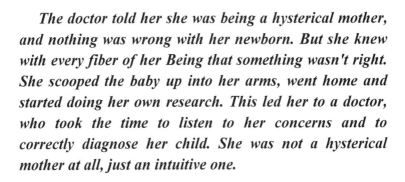

The doctor told her she was being a hysterical mother, and nothing was wrong with her newborn. But she knew with every fiber of her Being that something wasn't right. She scooped the baby up into her arms, went home and started doing her own research. This led her to a doctor, who took the time to listen to her concerns and to correctly diagnose her child. She was not a hysterical mother at all, just an intuitive one.

He had a choice to make. Two employers had offered him a summer job. The first one paid more money, but the energy around it felt cold and flat. The paycheck at the second job would be less, but the people who worked there seemed warm and caring. He took the second job and met a man who became a close friend. That supportive relationship lasted over fifty years and enriched his life.

I had walked to my car after work for five years. This evening I felt uneasy. I kept trying to reassure myself that all was well. Nothing looked different, yet I could not dismiss that feeling to be aware and on guard. I told myself I was being childish and should just shake off my uneasiness. As I got closer to my car, a man jumped out from behind a van, grabbed my purse and ran. I was fortunate that I wasn't hurt. This was a good lesson in paying attention to my God-given gift of intuition.

He was boarding an aircraft when panic washed over him. He feared that the plane could crash. Taking a minute to consider whether the uneasiness was coming from his mind or was a warning from his soul, he was able to feel that the trepidation was only in his mind. His brain was replaying movies of plane disasters. In his soul, his chest area, he was calm and clear.

When you take the time to use your tools along with what you have learned in your life, you can save yourself quite a bit of anxiety and wasted moments. Don't confuse intuition with your mental process. Intuition comes from the knowing of your soul, not the thoughts of the mind that can also contain fear or the emotions of the heart.

My house was for sale. The kids had grown up and moved on with their lives, leaving me with a huge home to manage. It was on the market for a few days when realtors began calling to make appointments to show it to potential buyers. I gave each room an extra cleaning, hung fresh towels in the bathrooms, and lit a few candles to make the house feel cozy. As I was walking towards my stereo to turn on soft music, I heard a well known song playing in my mind, "We all live in a yellow submarine." A somewhat lively and quirky song, I dismissed it and tuned the stereo to soft music, to create a relaxing environment.

After the potential buyers left, I blew out the candles and turned off the music. Again, I would hear "We all live in a yellow submarine," playing inside of me. Eight potential buyers later, I once again got the phone call from a realtor that she wanted to show my house. That day I listened to my inner guidance and put, "We all live in a yellow submarine" on the stereo. The clients bought the house that night— guidance or coincidence?

My personal experience with clairsentient ability was hit or miss, and I never knew which it would be. In trying to sense the energy around me, I would invariably step into it and take in energy that was not mine. I would find myself with a convoluted sense of self, creating a false sense of knowing. I was most comfortable with my clairvoyance and utilized and tended toward using that gift with passion and gratitude.

As a child, I saw things that were not physically evident, mostly fleeting movement when darkness fell. I believed that I would outgrow it, as no adult I knew admitted to seeing anything frightening.

At twenty-two years of age, when I saw the small boy in my hallway with my inner vision and through my physical eyes, I was seeing another dimension with both my inner and outer sight at the same time. As I pursued knowledge and control of this skill, I refined my ability to see, and then learned when and how to shut it off.

Next came the pursuit of only witnessing what was in my highest good, and what was meant for me to know or process in the moment. That also meant learning to deal with shadow or darkness, so it would harm no one, including me. Protection was imperative, and I went straight to the top for advice and help. Michael the Archangel shared tools of protection with me, and when I fell short, he stepped in.

Archangel Michael taught me to align myself with God, which meant I stood solidly in a Beam of the Creator's Light. Before I offered to help other people with my gift, I asked Angels to surround me and received permission from the Creator. I intended to have unrelenting courage, to never back down to evil, to be willing to stand between malicious energy and the person who came for my assistance and for my aura to be brilliant and strong. My stance became, No Fear.

Soon, other people began to ask me to sit and share my ability with them. Again, I learned to change channels to their energy vibration by shifting my focus. My switch involved asking the person to state their full names—each full name they used in this lifetime. In saying their name, they gave me permission to look at them and most often, this act would alert me to look at a particular part of their life.

For example, if a woman said, "My name is Shana Alise White" (her maiden name), "Shana Alise McCourt" (her married name), I either saw an image of her, or one of the names would stand out. In this instance, the name was printed out in a straight line, but her middle name, Alise, was shown fractured and shoved downward. I saw "MG" above it indicating the name was attached to her maternal grandmother. The energy of that relationship had deeply wounded Shana. I asked the Light for more information. I saw her grandmother in my mind's eye, mistreating Shana when she was a child. It had left Shana feeling unworthy of love. That is the first thing we worked on until that part of her was cleansed and healing.

Each step took me closer to refining my gifts. It brought me to a new level of knowledge and wisdom about the state of the soul that I did not know we had available to us in Earth School. I discovered a connection with other souls and Light that I never knew existed.

I began to embrace my Earth School education with my entire Being. It brought to my life limitless wealth in the experience of the Unity of Souls. In seeing the path of thousands of souls and witnessing their courage and personal stories, I became more compassionate and gained a deeper understanding of the Universe. In following my soul path, I became a strong Advocate for all souls that found their way to me. My desire is to support and encourage each soul as they search for answers in their life.

The energetic talents of spirit are discarded tools, unless you use and incorporate them into your life. Clairvoyance is disregarded, unless you open the eyes of your soul. Seeing with your inner eyes is just a picture unless you act to understand it and how it applies to your soul journey. Clairaudience is just noise until you decide who and what to listen to. The clairsentient ability and intuition are just curiosities until you take time to comprehend their value. Telepathic communication ends when directed at you, unless you are open to receive it, understand the skill, and learn when and how to use it.

Consider honoring the talents that you were blessed with, and have gratitude for the time and place in which you can strengthen and grow in those talents.

Some people possess all these energetic gifts equally. However, in most cases, one ability will show up as predominant, and the remaining abilities will range from strong to non-existent. Do not waste your time and energy wishing you had one of the gifts you do not hold. This takes time and power taken away from the talent you do possess. It would be like wishing you were taller, when you can't be.

For example, if you were physically blind, you would commonly find that your hearing was sharper than normal, to compensate for the loss of sight. And so it can be with your energetic skills.

Gifts of Spirit

Let's examine more gifts of Spirit available to you while you are in Earth School:

Love. The enormous gift of Love lifts our souls, brings us together and moves us to be greater than we ever thought possible.

Time. Without the precious gift of time in Earth School, we would not have the same opportunity to learn or grow. Use your moments wisely. We truly spend our minutes here, just as we spend our money. You have only so much, so spend it mindfully. Are you using your time fruitfully by appreciating the opportunity of the present moment or wasting it by dwelling on what happened yesterday?

I have heard many Students, especially seniors, wonder, "Where did all the time go? It went so fast." Perhaps they would have managed their lives differently had they consciously realized they were limited. Pay attention to the moment so you do not miss it. One of the finest gifts you can give to another person is the commodity of your time and focus.

One man understood the importance of time and made spending quality hours with the people in his life a priority. He decided to call family and friends who lived out of town every few weeks. He gave at least an hour a day of undivided attention to his child and quality moments to his wife every evening. He dropped by to see his parents on the weekend and regularly put moments aside for himself. He recognized that days go by quickly, and then, the attention you wished you had spent on valuable action is gone.

Another man was so consumed with his needs, that he gave little or no attention to anyone else. He did not understand that what his family and acquaintances hoped to receive from him was his interest in them. For him, claiming that his own life and work took all of his time was easier. In his mind, he did not have one moment to call and simply say, "I was thinking about you. How are you?" The message he sent was, "I am too busy with me to spend my valuable moments with you."

A third man was goal-driven. He listed his objectives on his wall. Once a goal was achieved, he checked it off and went on to the next. His list looked like this: graduate, marry, buy a house, have two children (one boy and one girl), earn a salary of $100,000 per year by age thirty.

But remember, in making the choice, he had to accept the consequences. In reaching his goals, he had not allotted time to give attention to the health of his completed achievements. All of his energy and focus were turned towards the next goal. He provided the material things for his family, but not what they truly needed from him—his time and interest.

Maintain the gifts you already have in your life by giving them time and attention, if you wish to keep them healthy and vibrant. Remember the purpose of life, and do not let life control you.

Prayer and Meditation. The power of prayer and meditation gifts us with health and well-being. They can help you unite all your components with a Higher Power. They quiet the mind, connect you to the soul, center you and provide comfort and guidance.

Curiosity. Curiosity represents an open mind and is a gift to motivate you forward to seek out what is possible.

Free will. Free will provides the offer of choice. It is one of the most important gifts and at the same time, one of the most difficult to balance. With conscious practice, this gift allows each individual a unique soul journey.

Free will allows you to define your true self. You can follow what society dictates or follow your own soul's path. The two may intersect many times. Will you choose what your culture expects, or the course of the journey you have chosen? Free will allows you to choose in every second, how to live your life in all of your aspects—physical, emotional, mental and spiritual.

Here are some questions to consider:

- Will you allow someone else to take your free choice?
- Will you try to control someone else?

Domineering people appear in all areas of life. They try to dictate everything, from your hairstyle to where you should live. They might bombard you mentally about what to think, how you should act, and then judge what is successful by their standards.

Spiritually, many of you were told what to believe, who to pray to and what rules you must follow. We will all experience judgments from other Students who will debate about who is right, and who will be condemned for their beliefs. Religion and spirituality are not necessarily the same.

Free will is one of the first lessons many souls review when they return home. You can gauge how well you honored your personal gift of choice and how much you respected the opinion of others.

Think about that for a moment. If you allow someone else to make your decisions for you, or bow to their suggestions and demands, instead of honoring your own path, will you live a life of intention? Fulfill your needs, travel your life path, and accomplish your goals.

There was a man who told his children where to live, whom to marry, what job to take, and how they should think. Nearly every decision went through him. He dictated their lives.

They did not summon the courage to stand up to their father and live their own journey, so they meekly deferred to his demands. His family chose not to spend the few moments of discomfort they would have experienced to confront their father, and opted instead for a lifetime of paternal control.

Try to avoid the mistake of influencing or taking charge of another's free will. Many Students think they know how to fix someone else's life, rationalizing that they can see more clearly what is best from the outside. However, if you are not asked for your opinion, help, or advice, and you interfere anyway, you might be taking away the entire reason people are in School—to learn from their circumstances for themselves. Attempting to fix someone else could harm both of you.

Altogether, your gifts and tools can provide you with more avenues for attaining knowledge and soul growth.

Physical tools

Just as people have evolved, so have their physical tools. Not that long ago, news and stories were passed by word of mouth, generation-to-generation. Wisdom and information were shared slowly over time. That has changed drastically. With the introduction of computer technology, you have access to most information with a few strokes on a keyboard. Incorporating physical tools, like computers, into everyday life gives you the opportunity to accomplish more in a shorter period. Learning how and when to use them can save hours of grueling, manual labor.

Here are a few more of the innumerable physical tools available to you in Earth School:

Your Smile. Your smile is a fabulous gift. Not only will your brain release endorphins when you smile, it will

217

attract similar energy towards you. Smile in gratitude and in pleasure, smile to enhance your existence and then share it with others. A simple grin can create interaction and support amongst your fellow Students. A smile is a great tool for enhancing and attracting positive energy.

Weather. Another gift is the changing weather. As with all gifts, it can affect you—physically, emotionally, mentally, and spiritually. You will each have your own reaction. Weather can save a farmer's livelihood or take it away. The climate can cause the ocean to rise and wreak havoc with civilization, or be the perfect place for a family vacation.

Some rainy days will be just right for a rest, and others will be inconvenient. The sun on your skin can be warm and inviting, or harsh and devastating. All weather is a gift. It reminds us that everything changes, and new lessons are right in the present moment. Weather is a great teacher of flexibility and adaptation.

Clean water. Clean water was a gift in great abundance in fresh rivers, clear lakes and healthy oceans. However, these resources have not been managed well by some Students, who are polluting or wasting this gift. Now pure water is sold in bottles, while other Students, who are concerned about the environment, work to resolve this problem. If the Student body continues to neglect the gifts of the Earth, how much longer will it be before the population is purchasing clean air to breathe, too? Consider this problem an opportunity to fix what is broken.

The Earth. The Earth itself is a gift, providing you with shelter, company, nourishment, tranquility and lessons in change. Every tree, hill and valley is a gift of beauty. However, remember, for every action there is a reaction. Cutting down too many trees will affect the air, the Campus, and eventually, the human body.

Tears. Tears are a gift that allows you to release toxins and express emotion. They are cleansing to the eye as well as the soul.

Colors. Colors are gifts that surround us every day. Color is not only a big part of the School Campus, but the entire Universe. Color and the energy it creates can be awe-inspiring, soul illuminating and soothing to the body.

Here are some examples of how colors can affect us:

Pink symbolizes unconditional feminine care, concern and love. Not surprisingly, as a society, we wear pink ribbons to show our support for the fight against breast cancer.

Yellow contains the energy of joy and the openness of possibility. If someone is sad, surround them with light yellow—flowers, clothing and sunshine. It will likely bring about a change.

Red has a vibrancy that can rouse more energy. If you put a person in a room that is all red, they will most likely become energized and possibly, over-stimulated. Used as an accent, red has a less lively effect. Dark red is commonly used as strong energetic protection.

Orange can promote togetherness, but at its darkest shade, it can signal fear. Every color has degrees of energy, depending on the shade, from the deepest to the lightest of hues.

The Earth is not predominately green and blue without intention. Green is nurturing and represents growth and healing. Blue promotes peace and stimulates spirituality. These colors encourage you to evolve and grow.

Cosmic Gold is a powerful energetic color. It consists of all of the colors of the Universe in translucent form, with striations of glimmering gold woven throughout. Students who are clairvoyant can see this color using their gift and others can intend for it to be present. This color can transmute whatever energy is present into one that is the most gracious for everyone. Intend for Cosmic Gold to be present when you want your words, environment and the atmosphere to show compassion for each individual. On the highest levels of Light in the spiritual dimensions is a Golden City of Light, inhabited by enlightened souls and formed entirely of Cosmic Gold. Imagine existing in a city where all things, even the air, is Cosmic Gold with a frequency that is perfect for each unique Being.

Cosmic Silver is another influential energetic color. Like Cosmic Gold, its tones are composed of all the colors in the Universe, but with striations of glistening silver. Cosmic Silver is very effective in soothing the nervous system of the human body. This color encourages peace and balance in spirit, mind and body.

Protection

We learn as children to protect ourselves in the physical world. The majority of us live inside a structure with walls, windows, doors and locks that provide protection.

We automatically protect our eyes from the bright sun. If heavy smoke fills the air, we shield our noses. If something is too hot or cold, we do not touch it. If sound is too loud, we cover our ears. We push away food that tastes bitter. The same can be said for emotionally devastating experiences. If you allow them to occur repeatedly, without taking steps to protect yourself, the damage can build and harm you emotionally.

Mental protection arises from life experience and understanding. Throughout your stay in Earth School, you learn to discern whom to spend time with, whom to avoid, whom to stand up to and whom to love for your well-being. As you establish financial stability, joy and balance in your life, you gain the protection of mental peace.

Protecting yourself from the critical voices in your mind by learning to quiet and eliminate them can help you feel and hear your soul instead. Strive to silence the voices in your brain so you can feel your soul. Use your brain as it was meant to be used, as a part of your body that is a tool for your soul. Altogether, protecting yourself on all levels, will help to bring balance to your life, thereby protecting your intended life journey from unnecessary interference.

You want to protect yourself when you use your energetic gifts, too. What energy or Being is putting that picture, thought, sound, intuitive feeling or telepathic communication around you? Is it originating from your soul, outside interfere, or guidance from a Light source? Allow nothing to invade your space without your permission. Check out the energy and Being before taking their advice. One way to do this is to ask them if they are in the Light, before considering what they present to you.

Allow life to flow around you, not through you.

Learn to protect the whole of you in all of your aspects. Make protection part of your everyday practice, as it creates a more comfortable and gracious way to walk through life. It is also a good lesson in self-awareness and strength of spirit.

Protective Aura

Shield your energetic self just as you protect your physical self. On the energetic level, your aura, which might also be referred to as your space or energetic structure, provides protection for your emotions, mind and connection to Spirit.

Your aura is the space around your body. It starts from your skin and extends out into the air surrounding you.

We all have an aura, but without our attention, it can become damaged. This happens when strong hurtful energy is pointed at us from any dimension. We can use our energetic structure as the foundation from which to build and strengthen our protection. To build your aura, intend that it be a specific color, size and vibration of energy.

To get a better sense of the aura, picture your physical body. Now imagine a hard-boiled egg. Your physical body is like the yellow of the egg, down in the middle, and surrounded by the white of the egg. You can intend that the white of the egg be a beautiful shade of green. Envision that it be light and airy, rather than solid like an egg white, and that the aura gently turns around your body in a clockwise motion.

Positive energy moves clockwise in an aura, and negative energy flows counter-clockwise. If your aura moves counter-clockwise, you might experience feeling anxious or wound up. Intend for it to change direction so you are held in positive energy. If you feel drained or exhausted without a tangible reason, you probably have a hole in your aura. Intend that your Guardian Angel hold you in protection, drop the torn energy structure and intend that a new one takes it place. You choose the colors and the layers of protection.

The shell of this egg, or your aura protection, is strongest when a vibrant protection color, such as cobalt blue, emerald green or vibrant ruby red is in place. You decide what feels right for you in that moment and circumstance.

Practice using different colors to find the ones that work best for you. You might find that a yellow aura with a rich red shell works best when you are at work. Perhaps lime green with an emerald green shell supports you when you experience illness. You decide what is best for you in every moment, and change your aura as many times as you wish.

Here are more tools to build your aura. Gather or create the energy you choose to surround yourself. You might choose strong protection, the gentlest of love or maybe even both. You decide what you want, intend for it to be so, feel it, picture it and just ask your Angel if you want help. Your Angel always stands at the ready. By taking charge of your space, your protection and the energy that surrounds you, the stronger and more empowered you become. Just as you will have varieties and degrees of protection on the Campus you have different forms of auras to protect you on an energetic level. Use pink to surround yourself with unconditional love and blue to encourage clarity and peace. Each life event can be enhanced by the protection will you place around you.

Before moving into difficult situations, prepare your aura in a protective manner that will not allow any person or outside energy to permeate your Being. Again, your intent alone will make it so. You can reinforce your intent by wearing a color that reminds you of your objective. Then, visualize your aura, see it with your inner vision, insist on it, feel it in your skin, know it in your soul and most importantly, practice and strengthen your abilities. As you see and feel the results, this protection can become a natural part of your everyday life.

As Students on the Earth Campus, you have probably experienced having ill-intended people direct cruel language or actions towards you. There are occasions this may shake you to your very core. However, a month later, those same individuals might say something even more malicious, and you will have little or no reaction. Why is that? What changed? The answer is the energetic protection you did or did not have around you.

Imagine that your physical body is standing in front of me. You have intended that a light yellow aura gently swirls around you, filled with the energy of joy. The chosen color of protection for the shell of your aura is cobalt blue. To add even more security, you can ask your Guardian Angel to stand in front of you.

Now, if I said something spiteful to you, my tone of voice, words, actions, and the look on my face, would leave my space and move toward you. As, as my mean energy flowed toward you, it would have come to your Angel, who is pure positive Light and Guardian protection. If my negativity could even penetrate the protection your Angel gave you, the sharp energy would be buffered before it reached you. Next, my energy would reach your protection layer of vibrant cobalt blue, where once again, it would be blocked or softened by your aura shell. Then, if it could still proceed forward, it would need to go through the light yellow power of joy you had placed as your aura. By the time any of my negative energy reached you, if at all, the sting of the barb I sent would be gentler and lighter.

This can also occur when one person sends energy to another from a distance—such as the hurtful energy sent through the words they have chosen to write in a letter or speak on the phone.

Seasons of Life and Soul

Each season on the Earth Campus brings different lessons and mirrors what can support the health of your mental, emotional and spiritual parts.

During the winter months, as the earth rests and waits, people tend to do the same. They are inclined to become more introspective and contemplate what is to come. On a soul level, you receive new lessons from your Higher Self for the New Year. Many people look forward to this fresh chapter and others struggle to maintain balance.

Spring brings rain showers, pollination, new foliage and a time to enjoy the outdoors after the long winter months. Students connect to the Earth more during this period, working on the land, exploring the landscape and enjoying their surroundings.

Spring can also present you with a new start and a new perspective on your journey. The lessons of spirit you received in the winter continue to unfold and weave into your everyday life. Spring cleaning can help clear room for that process. As part of it, you can also mentally and emotionally clear out old wounds, beliefs and toxic thoughts.

Summer is a season of warm weather and offers the chance to relax, and to balance work and play in your life. Your lessons that appeared in the winter will become more evident during this period, giving you the opportunity to learn all you can about each subject. This time is yet another opportunity to finish what you haven't completed from your winter Classes. Your Higher Self will present those lessons again to you in a more obvious way, accompanied by a sense of urgency to prepare you for the fall season.

In the fall, just as the trees lose their leaves, and the earth prepares itself for the winter months, so do the Students on Campus. With lessons still to recognize, work on, refine and complete from the winter, practicing the responsibility to self is important. Keeping current with the lessons your Higher Self is sending to you, prepares you for the next step in your education. New lessons come in every winter and the process of attending new lessons begins again.

Autumn can be an opportune time to cleanse your mental aspect of what is in the past, or to release emotional ties that no longer serve a purpose. Purging allows new space within all the parts of you and helps you move forward on your journey, rather than staying stuck in the past.

As each season passes and brings new opportunities for growth and learning, you have the chance to become more enlightened, more fully yourself, and to gain wisdom.

Reach Out and Ask

Consider using another tool that you can access on the Earth Campus. This is the powerful tool of reaching out and asking for help. Many of us are on the path together, trying to face our fears and strengthen our courage and resolve.

Here are a few more reminders of how to utilize this tool most effectively:

- Just ask. Try to remember that. Just ask. You are not alone. You have people, souls, and guides to help you and the Creator will always listen. While asking for help is important, remember too that you are in Earth School to learn to become strong and wise as you create your life. If you ask God or other people to do everything for you, what would you learn?

- Students tend to fear what they do not understand. Consider learning all that you can from as many teachers as possible. Do not let fear prevent you from becoming all you can be.

- Our human world is filled with teachers, advisors and friends. On a human level, just ask someone for help when you need assistance. You can do the same in the energetic sense. Ask your Angel or your Higher Self, Spirit Guides, Protectors, Healers—all the way to the Creator for help and answers. Some answers from this realm appear in your human world as a book or picture with a particular message. Sometimes it is a person who appears to offer the support you require.

- Making use of your energetic gifts along with your physical abilities can provide you with more help and assistance as your life moves forward. Use the tools that your School has to offer and the gifts of spirit to help navigate through your courses and journey.

- If you are uncertain of who you are or of your purpose in life, ask yourself, "What would I choose to be or do?" Then move in that direction and more clarity will come to you.

- Use all your gifts to be aware of signs and symbols that lead you forward in a positive way. Once you are aware you are in the presence of a sign, confirm it's origin, then be still and listen to receive its message.

- Remember that you are a soul on the Earth Campus who has been given the tools of the body—hands, feet, mind, and emotion, to help you in your School education. Use your tools. Keep them sharp, clean and efficient. But also know that while your physical tools can assist, they are never the definitive you. When you lay them down, your eternal soul will be left standing.

Consider using all of your gifts in harmony.

- See with your physical eyes

- See with your inner vision what is not evident

- Hear with your physical ears

- Hear the inner voice of your soul and receive guidance

- Taste and smell with all of your senses

- Breathe in what is beneficial

- Exhale what is toxic

- Know with your intuition

- Communicate with your energy

- Feel from a soul level

Be An Empowered Soul

Distractions

And

Illusions

What did you see— What were you told

Is it Your Truth?

The path to enlightenment can be filled with distractions and illusions. A distraction is anyone, any thing or any place that diverts your attention from your intended journey. An illusion is something that appears to exist, but in reality does not. Both can overshadow your present moment. Stay focused on the true lesson in the moment, not distracted by how it is being presented to you.

Distractions and illusions exist as part of your Classes and lessons to give you the opportunity to strengthen your fortitude, sharpen your focus and rise above nuisances to become the best you can be. What will you create when faced with a distraction or illusion?

Some of the distractions and illusions you encounter in School are obvious, while others are not so apparent. A number of people live their entire lives preoccupied with the disruptions around them, rather than focusing on their true soul intention. When that happens, they have difficulty focusing on the true lesson in the moment.

Many Students on the Earth Campus may appear as if they are perfectly fine on the outside physical level. However, conflict, confusing thoughts and negativity may twist their insides. Emotional confusion, mental anguish or spiritual collapses are not always evident. These illusions usually begin in the mind and work their way into the emotions.

Distractions can catch the attention of the mind by bombarding it repeatedly with outside images. Many images focus on criticism that belittle or add to your fear. Once the mind goes into fear, emotion follows. In turn, fear can affect the well-being of the physical body.

What choice will you make? Will you choose to live distracted by inner conflicts or strive to be present in the moment and build upon the true intent of your time in Earth School? Will you allow illusions of the outside world to divert you from living in reality?

Live from your soul
and not in your mind,
and all things are possible.

Here are a few examples of common distractions and illusions:

Racing Thoughts

Part of your Earth School education is learning to balance the partnership between your body, mind and soul. One challenge to this balance is racing thoughts that can run through your mind without conclusion or resolve. Some thoughts re-play past events. Others focus on fear of potential future situations. Racing thoughts are a loop of disconnected presumptions that swirl and rumble in your mind. Unchecked, they allow your mind, a part of your body, to move to the forefront of your Being, where it can control the whole of you.

This common occurrence can provide the opportunity to recognize the problem, overcome it, resolve racing thoughts and live your life in the peace of knowing you are growing. These events will encourage you to take control of your reactions to outside disruptions and create something positive from a negative. Once you do, you will benefit by being better able to connect with your Being. Your soul can be difficult to hear, feel or connect to, when it competes with racing thoughts.

Ali found herself going room-to-room trying to organize her belongings. At the same time, her mind was running at full speed, becoming overwhelmed. It jumped from worrying about the future, to reviewing wounds of the past and becoming anxious about the tasks at hand.

As she moved items from one room to the next, Ali found that she was not creating new order, but only shifting disorder to another place. By the end of the day, she had accomplished nothing except creating more frustration. In truth Ali's soul was hoping to learn more about orderliness and contentment. The lesson was not learned that day.

Cara took her seat on the bus and noticed the man sitting across from her. From the outside, he appeared to be a pleasant person, perfectly content, and she concluded he must be happy. However, inside his dialogue was raging as thoughts rushed through his mind, "How dare they ridicule me. I am smarter than most people could ever hope to be. One person after another has ruined my life. Why do they all go after me? Life is so unfair. I am just miserable living with all these stupid people. They do not value my opinion. They were lucky I even took their crummy job."

Stop Racing Thoughts. The next time you become aware that thoughts are racing through your mind, take steps to stop them. One method to bring yourself into reality is by noticing what is in your immediate present. Name what you observe. "I am sitting on a gray vinyl seat on the bus, and all is well around me. I am in no danger and give my full attention to this moment." When thoughts race through your brain, remember to purposely say:

"These are not my intended thoughts,"

until your mind is quiet.

Faulty Thoughts And Thought Forms

Faulty thoughts are not founded in reality. They are based on irrational thinking that has formed into opinions. They also provide another Earth School opportunity to learn for the enlightenment of your soul.

Recognize Faulty Thoughts. Do not believe everything you think. Just because you have a thought does not mean it is true. I call faulty thinking, "stinkin' thinkin'."

Consider these examples:

"If I don't make this much money, my family can't survive."

"I don't know why God keeps punishing me."

"My job is to make my family happy."

"I can tell by the way you look at me that you don't like me."

"If I love him, he will love me back."

"My life is a mess because of what other people did to me."

"I am too old to learn."

"School is too difficult."

"Life is unfair."

Consider what that thinking produces. What you think about expands. You have a choice. Your life and perspective will transform when you change faulty thinking. Don't take away time from your School experience by wasting it on negative thinking.

Try these thoughts instead:

"I'm grateful for my life and the chance to make good choices."

"God does not punish. These experiences are just Classes giving me the opportunity to learn."

"I empower myself to be happy and encourage you to do the same."

"I will smile when you look at me."

"I love him."

"My life is my responsibility that I embrace."

"Every moment provides me with opportunities."

"This School is perfect for my growth."

"Life is about learning and creating."

Thought forms are ideas that take shape in your mind, regardless of reality. As that thinking becomes ingrained in you, it can affect your life journey as you respond to imagined circumstances, rather than what is real and present.

Recognize Thought Forms.

"I thought life needed to be hard in order for it to be profound."

"I thought if I gave you all my time and attention, you would love me."

"I thought if I married outside of my race, my children would suffer."

"I thought if I drove an expensive car, I would feel powerful."

Karina attended Earth School to learn as much as possible in the Courses of Love, Communication and the essence of Wholeness. This is part of her story:

Karina had three healthy children who grew into independent adults. One by one, they started their own lives and moved away. That made her feel lonely, and she didn't like to be alone.

There had been complications with the birth of her fourth child, Steve. He was born without the ability to hear or speak and had a slightly diminished mental capacity. All the doctors recommended he be sent to a school for the hearing impaired to learn to communicate and interact with the outside world. They were confident that one day, he would be able to live on his own.

Karina thought about that option for a long time, and concluded that if Steve could communicate with others, someday, he would leave her and build his own life. Her thought form that being alone was the worst possible circumstance began to grow. She became determined never to be lonely again. Karina was living in a manner that filled her time and took her attention, but it was not for the illumination of her Being.

She convinced herself that she and her son would both be happiest if they had each other, without any outside interference. She decided to keep Steve home. Together, they began to use sign language that only they understood. Not even the family knew what the hand signals meant.

Karina thwarted any attempt by social workers or relatives to work with her son and kept him to herself for forty-two years. Then, when she died, he was left in a world of silence where no one understood him.

Now that she has graduated from the Earth Campus, Karina is carefully reviewing the decisions she made as a Student. She is disappointed that she lived in fear of what could happen rather than the perspective of the reality presented by her Classes. Attempting to learn positive lessons from negative or selfish actions is now her priority.

Steve now lives with other Students who are challenged in similar ways. On a soul level, he has gathered a great deal of wisdom in several unusual areas that he will add to his Being. Steve lived a controlled life with his mother and is now creating a new life of positive interaction with his new friends.

Ninety percent of everything we fear will not happen.

How much energy will you spend reacting to something that may never occur?

Voices That Do Not Belong

A voice heard from without or within that cloud the truth, belittles or distracts you, is a voice that does not belong. Learning how to deal with these voices and not letting them run your life is a common course in Earth School.

Imagine living your life with a bully walking alongside you. His only purpose is to create negativity. With his words, expression and voice tone, he attempts to drag you down and create oppressive energy. The inner and outer chaos that ensues affects your existence by distracting you from your true self, thoughts, intentions and life creation. Would you allow this tormenter to follow you everywhere, day and night, or would you put a stop to it?

With a tyrant by your side as a source of stress and irritation, how could you sleep peacefully, share a pleasant moment or even *be* in the moment? Could you be a partner in a loving and supportive relationship? Would it be possible to embrace your journey at all? Chances are your top priority would be to stop the harassment. You would use all the options and tools available to you to stop this type of interference and abuse on all levels, and claim your space and right to peace.

Stop listening to the voice of your inner bully by learning to recognize the voice of your soul instead. It resonates from your solar plexus, not your mind. Identify voices from the shadows that may cause you to falter or the voice of the unknown that demeans you. Perhaps the voice will be that of a teacher, who tells you that you are stupid, or of a tormentor, who yells obscenities at you. "You are not smart." "You are not attractive." "You are not good enough." "What is wrong with you?" "I was only kidding." "You are too sensitive." "You are lucky I put up with you." Words that devalue you, in any manner, should be silenced. This is part of your Earth School curriculum.

Make living in your soul a priority and create peace in your mind.

Belief Systems

A belief system is something you believe, regardless of reality. These systems take away your free will. Held within your Being, they can appear on physical, mental, emotional and spiritual levels. They are energy you carry, believe and act upon, without conscious thought.

You have an alternative. Choosing every minute to do what is in your highest good is better than acting or reacting in a set way, because you believe you must.

Gather all the wisdom you can and discipline your thinking to identify and alleviate Belief Systems, so they no longer dictate your life.

Ann had never witnessed the type of love connection she wanted in her life where the couple experienced lasting mutual respect, love, understanding and encouragement. To her, the most reasonable belief seemed to be that relationships were hard. She perceived that to be true, and thus, her belief system was set in place.

Instead of going after the kind of relationship she wanted, she let her belief system guide her and settled for the closest thing to acceptable in choosing a life partner. All the difficult times, discord and loud arguments that followed reinforced her belief that relationships are difficult.

Recognize Belief Systems. Some things are true whether you have experienced them or not. Forming a belief, that what you have not witnessed cannot exist, is simply another belief system.

For example, just because you have not had a certain type of positive connection in a relationship, does not mean you cannot create that relationship. Sadly, this belief system has caused untold numbers of people to settle for something less. In the end, their resentment about having settled reigns.

Belief systems create limits, and with those boundaries, you create your own reality. When you treat these beliefs as your truths, you live your life as if they were true—even when they are not. Discovering any belief systems that you gauge your life with is also part of the courses offered on the Earth Campus. Learning how to eradicate them, so you can live the life you select for the highest good of your soul is important.

Tara believed she would die young, like the women in her family had done before her. As a result, she lived her life as if an early death for her was a given. Taking unwise risks and not building a foundation became her way of being. Because she did not intend to have a future, "Why not?" became her mantra. If you believed you had no future, what life foundation would you build?

Kate loved her father dearly and sometimes, she could see pride on his face when he looked at her. His temper always came as such as surprise to her. One minute all was well, and in the next moment, everything could change. She formed this belief system, "You are my father ... and you love me ... and hold me ... and hit me ... when I need it. When I grow up, I will choose a man who loves me ... and holds me ... and hits me ... when I need it, because that is how a male loves a female.

Kate lived her life around the moods of those around her, trying to appease chaotic people. Her Higher Self was hoping that she would realize she did not create those unacceptable events. She had not caused the abuse, nor could she change those who mistreated her. As she grew older and wiser, Kate discovered that what she could control was her reaction to circumstances and resolve to choose what was best for her. She could opt for what was healthy and positive—what would cause her to claim her right to peace and respect. After all, those are her Classes in Earth School.

Belief systems eliminate your opportunity to exercise your free will and experience each event as it truly is, rather than being stuck in what you believe it will be. You might wonder if a belief system can ever be a good thing. The answer is no. It always takes away your free will in the present moment when automatic judgment decides your actions.

Ken believed he had to be a computer analyst. He firmly stated, "This is the only job I will ever do," because he believed it was the single occupation he could be happy doing.

One evening a few friends swept him up in their plans to help at the local homeless shelter. Unexpectedly, he found himself working at a soup kitchen. At first, he felt superior to the people around him. He went so far as to say to his friends, "Why don't they just go get a job?"

However, as the evening progressed, and he became engrossed in the work at hand, he discovered that he had never felt so needed. That night he learned more about the journey of the soul than he had in his entire career. For the first time in his life, Ken felt part of something bigger than himself.

The experience opened a window to his Being, and he began to wonder what else was out there that he could be part of, and what other work he could do that would be meaningful. Ken let go of his belief system and opened his mind to the possibility that life held more than he had believed.

Millions of people on the planet believe they can only survive in one environment, do one particular job or be surrounded by certain people. With billions of choices, it would be unlikely that you could only live in one state of Being. As a result, developing a belief system that holds you to one way of living can stifle your existence and smother your soul. Do not limit your Earth School experience to an existence that is based on tunnel vision. Stay open to all the wonderful courses available on the Campus.

Judgments can also gain energy from belief systems, even the ones about yourself. An automatic judgment is like a path you have pre-selected.

Prejudice, an extreme form of judgment, stems from belief systems, thought forms and preconceived mindsets that devalue others. When we hold back the potential of one person or group, we hurt everyone, ourselves included. We prevent ourselves from living in the truth—which has no place for prejudice or any other judgment.

Liberate yourself from belief systems, so that each second, you are free to choose how you want to be and to move forward on your chosen path.

Exercise to Alleviate a Believe System. To rid yourself of a belief system, write it down on a piece of paper. Take a red pen and write *void* and *cancel* all over the paper, front and back. Tear it into tiny pieces intending it leave your mind, body and soul. Ask your Guardian Angel for help.

Another way to rid yourself of a belief system is to imagine putting it in a bubble. Then send it over the ocean or mountains and intend that it explode, harming no one.

A common question people ask on Campus is, "What would you do if you knew you couldn't fail?" When you get rid of belief systems, you get to find out. You are able to discover reality, instead of mindlessly reacting to preconceived ideas. Empower yourself to discover the truth of each moment.

Beliefs and judgments have been formed by society and passed on to the next generation, even though few Students can remember why or how they became an accepted truth. Still, believe the beliefs and judgments wholeheartedly.

I have heard people say, "We don't associate with those people, they will rob you blind." Another common phrase is, "They must be held back, or they will take over."

Stop and think before you speak from a place of judgment or belief. Draw boundaries to shield yourself from others beliefs and judgments. Reach your own conclusions.

Mindless expressions move ignorance forward. Beliefs that cause you to stifle the talents and abilities of any individual wound the entire planet.

Expectations of Society

Society presents us with millions of diversions and expectations. It has caused many of us to forget the reason we went to Earth School. We are in School to experience lessons and become more enlightened Beings, not to conform to outside restrictions. Do not let society's beliefs on how to live, look and think, deter you from your soul journey. See those expectations as a challenge to overcome on your road to becoming your authentic self.

Aspire to rise above the illusion that supporting your lifestyle is more important than living your life.

Don't live your life with cattle mentality— mindlessly following the rules of society. Instead, create your own existence, free from those influences. A large portion of the Student population focuses on the potential judgment of others—"What will they think? What will they say? Will I be ostracized if I don't do it their way?"

What makes Students so insecure when they are on the Earth Campus? Why do they struggle to get the approval of people, most of whom they do not know or respect? The search for outside approval comes when human desire overshadows the soul and is not healthy for any part of you.

Mariah believed what the media dictated. You must be tall, thin, tan and beautiful to have value. She was round

247

and soft and had short curly brown hair. Society led her to believe that she was not attractive, and so she felt she did not matter. With this information, she formed a belief system that since she did not meet society's standard of attractive, she would have to settle for whomever wanted to befriend her. Even if she did not feel a connection with that person, she would be grateful for anyone who accepted her.

Her parents countered the media and told Mariah she was here to be herself, and she was more than enough as she was. That alternative perception felt much better to her. It struck a chord in her soul. Mariah knew it was true, but she still questioned whom she would believe.

Jason and his wife, Mary, believed what society told them. Work hard, save and invest your money, and you will insure that your retirement years will be comfortable.

Therefore, they bought a modest home, went to $2.00 movies and brought their own popcorn. On Sundays, they clipped coupons from the newspaper and shopped for sale items. They bought affordable cars and kept them until they no longer worked. They gave their time and attention to their financial future.

Over the period of forty-five years, Jason and Mary saved a quarter of a million dollars. They were proud of saving that amount of money. They felt assured they would have enough funds to enjoy their golden years.

Unfortunately, the companies they invested in were run by people who took large multi-million dollar salaries, and those companies went bankrupt. Now their retirement money is gone. John and Mary's belief that if you live by the book, your life is guaranteed to be comfortable, proved not to be true. They feel deceived.

One day this couple will see that their best investment was in themselves. The ethics, morals, wisdom and intentions they gained in their years of living and working can never be stolen from them. Every sacrifice they made, the love they created and even the testing of their spirit is far more important than the state of their finances. After all, what will they take with them when they leave the Earth Campus? Money is not the currency of the soul.

Julia believed that marriage is forever, for better or worse, for richer or poorer. However, she and her new husband had not been married long before he became critical of her and let her know that her thoughts and needs held no value to him. In those moments, she learned to be quiet, almost invisible, by breathing slowly and softly.

He felt even more disdain for her when she withdrew, preferring that she fight back, so he would have more reason to explode and feel powerful. At least, she would be a worthy opponent. Then the day came that he pushed her down on the couch and verbally attacked her.

Nevertheless, marriage is forever, she rationalized, and she loved him and so she stayed.

The next time Julia mad made him, he pushed her into a wall, and her back was never the same. However, she loved him, and marriage is forever and so she stayed.

His drinking increased, especially on weekends, and his agitation grew with each can of beer he swallowed. He was outraged so often she began to lose track of the reasons why.

One Sunday afternoon she dared to ask him why he was angry. That enraged him so much he held a gun to her head, pulled back the hammer and then told her she wasn't worth it.

However, she had promised to love him forever and she had a belief that society frowned on divorce. They call it a failed marriage and she didn't want to fail. She believed God would judge her for breaking her vow, and so she stayed.

<hr />

Kevin believed if he applied himself, studied hard and got his degree, he would be well compensated in his working years. However, the economy fell apart, and he still owed $50,000 in student loans. He clung to his belief system that if he did his part, life would be fair, and everything would automatically fall into place. However, for now, he cannot get any job. Kevin has become angry about his past, uncomfortable in the present and hopeless *about the future. What would happen if he got rid of his belief and said, "Now what?" and began to live his life?*

⁓

Keith was an only child. For three generations, the men in his family had become powerful attorneys. They were proud to point out he would be the fourth generation. No one ever questioned the fact that he would take over the family law firm and continue the tradition.

In his second year of college, Keith met a man who asked him why he had chosen to study law. He did not know what to say. Actually, he had never thought about it before. It was a revelation to him that it mattered what he wanted. He acknowledged to himself he did not even like law. In his family, all that was important was winning the case, not that justice prevailed. Keith wanted no part of it.

Keith realized if he could be anything in the world, he would choose to be a carpenter. When he was sixteen years old, he had spent the summer with his cousin, working in his uncle's wood shop. There he discovered wood seemed to come alive in his hands. The aromas that filled the shop enhanced his senses.

Woodworking was his passion, and his gift was to create beautiful furniture. He embraced being physically tired at the end of a day. He went home feeling inspired, fulfilled and content.

Would he choose to disappoint his family or himself? What is his responsibility to his soul?

His mind went into fear when he considered what his family would say. Had he wasted the last two years in college? What if he could not support himself? What if...?

His emotions rolled up and down as he followed the fear in his mind. However, in his soul, Keith had discovered himself.

I encourage you to avoid developing new belief systems and to cancel any you already have. Exercise your free will to choose your thoughts, words and actions. Many of my accomplishments on Earth occurred because I did not know *it couldn't be done.*

Empower yourself to be who you are, knowing that every moment, you will move forward with confidence and strength.

Perfect Pictures

A perfect picture is a snapshot you carry in your mind of how you want an event or goal to turn out. Any condition that falls short of that image can feel like a failure or like the situation is not good enough. Building an ideal picture in your mind and making it your absolute goal will most likely set you up for failure. After all, what is perfect? The most likely outcome, when the flawless depiction does not present itself, is self-criticism or blaming another for ruining your goal.

Speak your truth, even if others do not understand. The planet needs you to be you. You are the only you who exists. You cannot be replaced or duplicated. There would be a void for all of us without you.

Illusions come with the energy of perfect pictures. They are not based in reality. Watch out for illusions because they create the *what if's*, which are notorious for getting souls stuck in only being happy if the illusion becomes a reality. Be happy now, in this second, in reality, fully present.

Examples of Perfect Pictures:

If I had that boat, then I would be happy

If we were perfect for each other, then I would be happy

If I got my degree, then I would be happy

If it didn't rain tomorrow, then I would be happy

If I wasn't fat, then I would be happy

If I didn't have to work anymore, then I would be happy

Unless those *what if's* happen, you have already decided you cannot be happy. Instead, you could choose to be happy now without the perfect picture. What a relief that would be.

Release Perfect Pictures. Close your eyes, and imagine a photograph of your perfect picture—every detail of it. Then intend to be holding scissors and snipping that photo into tiny pieces. Determine the pieces be burned in a violet flame. Ask your Guardian Angel to remove the energy of the perfect image from your body, wherever it is held. Intend for that part of you to heal.

Another way to release a perfect image from your mind is to be determined that this image leave your brain. Intend to tape that photo on a symbolic balloon, and release it to fly far away, over a desert or hill. When it reaches it's destination, it implodes and harms no one.

Happiness is not a perfect picture or condition. It is a state of Being.

They were ready to buy a house. Standing side by side in the two-story home, ignoring the anxiety beginning to build inside them, Gary and Jennifer smiled at each other. The house was out of their price range, but it was the one they had pictured—their perfect house. They decided to purchase it, a decision that would change their lives forever.

That one choice meant Gary would commute two hours to work each day. Jennifer would need to get a job to help pay the expenses and find day care for their nine-month-old son. Their budget would be stringent and extras would be cut. They would cancel their vacation, go out just once a month, and carefully shop only for what they needed.

The adventures that had bonded them would be replaced with stress and time spent away from each other and their son. In that house purchase, they changed their path from one of supporting their family relationship to supporting a lifestyle.

Jennifer and Gary put image and pride before the good of their family. However, they did not realize it in the moment they made their choice, because they could only see their picture perfect house. If they had chosen an affordable house, Gary would be home instead of navigating the highways for hours each workday. Jennifer could continue to stay home with their son, a role she embraced and in which he flourished. They could live comfortably, spend precious time together and save for their future.

Instead, they were carried away by the thought of owning this beautiful dwelling. They agreed to make it work and signed on the dotted line. The consequences fell into place, one by one. Financially strapped, overtired and with little time together, their process of growing apart began.

⸻

Shana was running herself and her children ragged overbooking their days. Their calendar, filled with appointments, play dates and lessons, was firmly taped to the refrigerator and ruled her days and their schedules.

Today, they can play tennis, guitar, baseball and soccer. However, they have little downtime to relax and play on their own or with each other. It did not occur to Shana to give the children time to invent games, stretch their imaginations and spend time together as a family.

Where was the balance? It did not exist. Instead, Shana and her husband were in debt, paying for their lifestyle, and their children felt disconnected and tired. Unfortunately, they are not an uncommon family.

Perfect pictures distract you from your true self, your personal journey and life flow. They divert your energy to something that does not exist rather than the creation of your life. Moreover, they prevent you from being happy unless the perfect picture is in front of you.

I encourage you to step back from your life routinely and examine your reality. See what Class or lesson is presenting itself to you. Let go of what you thought, and see what is. Then move forward into what is real and valuable. Review what you are actually creating with your life—repetitive action or creative interaction.

The truth is many people have spent their entire lives walking repeatedly into the same brick wall. Roadblocks only stop you if you let them. Go around, through or over them. Look to see what path you are missing and redirect your focus. That brick wall is there for a reason.

Change your perspective and accept what comes your way as a Class from which to learn. The world is not meant to be perfect, or what would you discover? I have seen people stuck their entire lives, upset about their imperfect world, trying to get everyone to cooperate and fit into their ideal portrayal of life. They bicker and complain when their perfect image appears to be messed up by someone else. They can become critical of those around them. "It must be their fault, surely not mine. Why is this happening to me?" The better question would be, "What can I create from this?"

Energetic Contracts

An energetic contract is an agreement between two or more people, which defines each person's obligation under the circumstances they outline. Energetic contracts can be agreed upon at any time—before birth, during Earth School attendance and after graduation. The arrangement means that rather than being able to exercise your free will in all situations, you will instead be required to fulfill that energetic agreement.

The same is true of everyone else involved in the contract. The contract will dictate the actions of all parties involved, regardless of free will or circumstance. Unfortunately, contracts do not always end up producing the most positive consequences. Souls enter into contracts thinking they will insure a specific outcome or all parties involved will gain something from the agreement. This is similar to situations on the Earth Campus when people enter into contracts to tie all parties into a specific action.

In both instances, you and the others continue to be tied to the contract even when it harms any or all of you. No further thought or consideration is required when a contract exists, just the automatic prearranged action.

"We will love each other every day and night until we die, no matter what. We will fulfill each other's needs or we have failed." This was a soul contract made between Lily and George when they agreed to marry.

Lily's voice was what first caught George's attention. As she stood in the middle of a crowded party, her laughter reached in and touched his heart before he ever saw her. When he finally made his way to where she stood, he knew he had found his soul mate.

Lily also remembers that party as a turning point in her life. George's interesting stories captivated her. She was impressed by his attention to detail. He could recount something that happened years ago without missing a single detail. She laughed so hard at his jokes, that sometimes she would beg him to stop. Her appreciation and attention made him feel proud and cherished.

George loved to listen to Lily sing. She sang when she woke up and when she was in the car. She sang while she cooked and made the bed. She had the voice of an angel, he said, and she felt so loved.

Then, one day he woke up not feeling well and could hear her singing in the shower. The sound made his head throb, and instead of appreciating her voice, he found he couldn't wait for her to leave for work.

When Lily came into the bedroom to kiss him goodbye, George looked at her as if he wanted her to be quiet, and her feelings were hurt. She went through her day at work upset at her husband. As a result, Lily came home in a bad mood.

In the meantime, George had begun to feel better and began telling her what had happened to the neighbors that day. Instead of appreciating his sharing, she found that listening to his stories, often repeated, was getting on her nerves.

He noticed the shift in her mood, especially when she didn't sing while she made dinner. That made him feel stupid. He had thought she liked his stories.

On that day, neither of them felt loved, and since they had a contract to love each other all the time, they felt betrayed and resentful. Now, they blamed each other for not acting lovingly. Without the contract, they would have been free to choose love in each moment, rather than feeling obligated to love. Instead of, "I have to love you," their commitment would have been, "I choose to love you." Rather than, "You are responsible for my happiness," their internal direction would have been, "I choose to be responsible for my happiness."

Do not expect to receive from people what they don't have to give. This behavior can get you stuck for years and potentially ruin your relationship. You can spend a lifetime expecting others to act in a particular manner, wondering why they don't meet your expectations. A wiser choice would be to see them clearly and accept them for who they are. Then decide how they fit, or do not fit, in your life. Be clear about what you choose to offer in a relationship and what the other person involved wants to give back. If you take responsibility for your own existence, what other people offer can be icing on the cake.

Girlfriends since college, friendship was important to Courtney, Dana, Brooke and Amy. They had an unspoken commitment that developed into an energetic contract with each other. "All for one and one for all. Leave no one behind. We will always be there for each other."

Two years after graduation, Amy met a man and stopped finding time for her friends. However, she did spend hours picking the perfect gift to send each of them on their birthdays and at Christmas. That was how Amy showed she cared.

Even so, Courtney, Dana and Brooke felt abandoned and began to speak badly of Amy. They didn't want a gift, they wanted Amy's time and attention. Sadly, they concluded they could not rely on her. After all, a good friend gave the gift of her time without being asked.

Brooke showed her love by preparing delicious meals for her friends. She routinely invited them to lunch, preparing their favorite dishes with great care. She spent hours chopping and sautéing, while anticipating the smiles her food would create.

On the other hand, Brooke was afraid of animals, so she would never consider caring for her friend's pets when they went out of town. They had to find someone else for that kind of help. Dana was upset by that, and began to believe Brooke wasn't such a good friend after all.

When her friends needed her, Courtney would come running, no matter what time or place. Just don't ask her to cook, because she did not know how and didn't care to learn. Brooke kept waiting for Courtney to reciprocate with a lunch invitation, but never got one. She concluded that Courtney was rude and inconsiderate.

Dana called her friends often and never hung up without saying, "I love you." They could always count on her for words of encouragement. She was a trusted confidant. However, Dana was always behind schedule and usually hours late. Her friends thought this behavior was disrespectful. Dana did not live her life by the clock and never thought much of it.

The four women expected from each other what they did not have to give, but they did offer what was theirs to share. Amy did not have time to offer, but showed her caring with gifts. Brooke nourished her friends with love and food. Courtney would come from the four corners of the Earth to stand with you. Dana was steadfast in her support.

To define friendship as all-encompassing was a contract sure to bring failure and disappointment. Consider being grateful for what friends and other loved ones offer and let go of contracts.

Souls can agree on contracts before leaving for Earth School. Here are a few examples:

Luke and Sara, a couple who had been married for eight years, came to see me, hoping to hear from a friend who had recently crossed over. As always, I began by asking Divine permission, that the four Archangels surround us with Light and that I do no harm. Then, I asked to be shown what was in their highest good to know or work through.

Their friend, Steve, came forward to tell me he had drowned while kayaking on the river. Luke, Sara and other friends who were on the river too that day, had gone to great lengths to try to save him, but were unsuccessful. Through me, Steve thanked Luke for trying so hard to rescue him and asked him to pass personal messages on to his family and other friends. He also confirmed to them that he was truly Steve by showing me personal items to relay to them.

Then, Luke and Sara received an unexpected insight from the session. I asked the Light if there was anything else I was supposed to see. I was shown the relationship aura held between the couple. It was small, dim and waning.

I asked what to do next. Their Guardian Angels moved in front of me and pointed to a small window up to my left. I was led to look through it. There, I saw Sara and Luke's souls before they were born in Earth School. They were agreeing to help each other during their life journey.

Sara's intentions were to attend Earth School to pursue wisdom for the part of her essence that concerned peace. She wanted to experience what disrupts peace, including anger. As part of this, she wanted to explore what causes rage, the degree to which it is expressed, when it is appropriate, the absence of it and what being the target of rage or the source of it felt like.

Luke wanted to learn as much as he could about all the aspects of tolerance—when to practice it and when to draw the line and have no more tolerance.

Their two souls agreed to help each other on the Earth Campus with their chosen subjects. Sara promised to test Luke's tolerance every day, to give him the chance to learn from the difficult lessons she would present to him. Luke promised Sara to support her in her endeavor to explore peace and its disruption.

All the opportunities fell into place and they were born in Earth School within a year of each other, met at work and married soon afterwards. As energetically promised, Sara tested his tolerance often, day after day, year after year. Luke served as the target of his wife's anger, and suffered so much from it that all of his strength went into simply existing. He had no reserve energy left for his other Classes.

Eight years later, they could see that living their lives around a contract that created negativity and impeded their free will in the moment was not in their highest good. This spiritual contract had harmed both of them, eroded their relationship and created resentment instead of growth.

Acting as an Advocate for their souls, I intended that the contract be put in front of them and instructed them symbolically to use a can of red spray paint and spray the word, VOID, on it. Then, they intended to hold a hammer and chisel and to break the contract in pieces.

Finally, we intended for the pieces to be burned with a violet flame, so they could harm no one. I was also shown where the energy of this contract had been held in their physical bodies. Sara's was held in the tailbone area (the first chakra). This is the area that holds the energy of how and where you live your physical life. Luke's contract energy was held in his head, and I could see that it created tangible pain in the form of headaches.

With the help of their Angels and Healers from the highest Light, that energy was carefully removed. The area was cleaned thoroughly to insure that not even one speck of contract energy would remain. Light aqua healing energy was added to expedite complete healing from the contract.

Next, we addressed their relationship aura. When this aura is healthy, I see both people standing facing each other. Between them is an egg-shaped energy that has a shell of bubble consistency. The color, brightness and size of the egg are a result of what the couple has put into the partnership. The top is usually just above their heads. The bottom is about six inches above the knee and a bit wider than the human body. In its most healthy state, both people have their hands mid-line on the egg to support and embrace what they are creating. They cannot see each other, because the egg blocks their vision. It is a matter of trust that the other person is still facing you, supporting the egg.

Sara only had her left hand on the egg and was looking over her shoulder. This told me she was receiving from the relationship, but not giving and was only half-

interested. (The left side is your receiving side, and your right side is your giving side. This is the way energy flows.)

Luke was bent over awkwardly, trying to balance the egg with both of his hands placed on the bottom of it. This told me he was feeling overwhelmed and in physical pain from the uncomfortable stance he held. Luke carried the weight of their relationship.

Looking into the egg, I could see bits of dull color, snapshots, crumpled trash and a hole in the back of the relationship aura, where most of the energy had leaked out. This represented what they had created together. It looked somewhat abandoned even though Luke still struggled to hold it up.

Sara and Luke wanted to begin again and live a better life together. Their Angels took the old aura up to their Higher Selves to be sorted through, and a new aura was placed between them. Now, they needed to decide what they wanted to put in the aura every second of every day— whether they wanted to hold and support their relationship or walk away. Knowing they have this relationship aura gave them greater focus on their path as a couple and as individuals.

Every relationship, between couples, parents, friends or siblings, has a relationship aura. Be mindful what you create in them.

Contracts that seemed like a good idea before you entered the Earth School can have a negative affect that takes away your free will, and in the end, accomplishes stagnation and frustration. Remember, you are in School to become wiser, not to act out contracts.

Here are a few more contracts I have personally witnessed between souls before they left for Earth School:

Daughter/Mother contract: "You will always support me, even when I'm wrong, and I will help you with your Class in stress management."

Father/Son contract: "I will make you a man, and you will be my son who pushes me to my limits to help me learn what I am capable of."

Siblings: "I will love you and stay in your life, even when you abuse me, because we are siblings."

Child/Parents: "You will be my parents, and I will take on your anger and fear, so you will stay together and continue to raise me."

Child/Mother: "You can create chaos and rage all around me, and I will stay because you gave me life."

"Wife/Husband: "You will financially support me, and I will provide you with affection, and children, and organize your home."

Relationships can be simple or complicated, but are usually a combination of both. Remember, you can only change yourself. You cannot change another person, no matter how hard you try. Every family, workplace or School Class seems to have at least one complicated relationship that tests everyone else in the group; the overly affectionate uncle, the inappropriate cousin, the hyperactive co-worker or the class bully. You may be taught to be careful not to upset these individuals, to monitor what you tell them, or not only you, but also everyone will be in for a rough time. Just keep them happy and calm, you are told, whatever that involves, even if you have to endure poor behavior.

Tina would beg her husband and children to ignore her sister's drinking at family gatherings. She expected them to overlook her sister's bad behavior as if it was not happening. This family silence had gone on for 10 years.

Finally, a child, one of the newest members of the family, who had only been alive for a fraction of that decade of family suffering, broke the cycle. The sister's three-year-old niece looked up at her aunt and announced, "Auntie, I think you need a time out." This child finally spoke the truth and drew boundaries creating the possibility of a better family dynamic.

Olivia and her cousins were told, "If you love your grandma, you will be nice to Uncle Bud and kiss him goodbye." Last year, Olivia was five years old when they visited Uncle Bud. When it was time to leave, he gave her a big, sloppy kiss. She looked up at him and said, "That was disgusting. You may never kiss me again." Her response was a wakeup call for the parents.

The louder and more bizarre the behavior from inappropriate people, the more attention they get. They become masters of manipulation, and yet the social expectation is often that you accommodate their unsuitable behavior.

Instead of letting contracts dictate your life, consider living a life of freedom. This means that you choose what is in your highest good in the moment. Decide what you love to do. This action will lead you to your passion and your purpose. Follow your soul, not a contract.

If you let someone else determine how you live, you might be letting him or her take away the reason you are in Earth School.

Whether contracts come from personal relationships or are set forth by the dictates and mores of societal relationships, like work and school, their impact on you can cause you to forget about the true purpose of your life.

Before making a change in their lives, many people wait, hoping for a feeling to magically change them without their having to take action. However, change does not come that way.

Instead, you need to make a decision, and that decision, not the feeling, will create the potential for change. Intending to move in your chosen direction will further create that possibility for transformation.

Remember what you are here on Earth to do. Diversions are everywhere in this world. Do not let the interruptions of the mind form your existence. Racing thoughts, belief systems, thought forms, faulty thoughts, outside voices, judgments and contracts can twist and build one upon another, until you find yourself overwhelmed without a starting place. The mind will tell you, "If this is true, then that must be true," and on it goes, until your life becomes based on the premise of distractions and illusions.

If you don't like it, fix it.
If you can't fix it, learn from it.

The peace of your mental aspect is extremely important to the whole of you. If you find yourself mentally distracted, pay attention and do what you can to rebalance and find peace. Perhaps thoughts of debt or guilt have filled your mind. Discover the problem and work on it until you resolve it. Living from your soul, rather than from your mental state, will bring peace.

Work hard to achieve emotional peace, too. Emotional upset is another signal to you that something in your life needs your attention. Do what is in your highest good for your emotional well-being. Release the fear of your emotions. They are reacting to mental thoughts and distractions and are not usually based in reality.

Distractions and illusions exist to give Students the opportunity to take what is negative and create something positive from it. Refuse to carry hate, participate in gossip, or act in a manner that is not your conscious choice and in your highest good. This creates harmony, clarity and purposeful energy.

Graduation

A new beginning—A time to reflect

A Celebration of Life

Many of you anticipate graduation as a new beginning and look forward to future growth. Most feel a sense of accomplishment and delight, happy to know they are adding illumination to their soul.

However, graduation can also bring mixed emotions. Leaving family, friends, teachers and the Earth Campus can feel bittersweet and requires stepping out of your comfort zone. Some of you see it as an ending.

Compare graduation from Earth School to that of high school or college. You have spent your last day as a student in your school. You and your friends will spread out to all parts of the world, never again to gather as you have for the past few years.

At the same time, you know you have completed that part of your life and are ready to move forward, to explore what awaits you, to start a new phase and apply what you have learned. Imagine what would happen if no one could bear to leave kindergarten. Society's growth would come to a halt.

When you graduate from Earth School, you do not leave with a diploma that prepares you for further study or a job. Instead, you hold the culmination of the energy you created through your experiences, thoughts, decisions and actions. Whatever anger, love, sarcasm or compassion you generated will become part of your essence. Many of you form a mixture of energies.

After graduation, you will find yourself present on an energetic level of energy—the plane of existence that best matches the energy you have created in the whole of your existence. Your Light, or lack of Light, is visible to every soul. It creates your vibration of energy. You will exist on the level that matches your vibration with other souls that have the same frequency.

Some astral souls, the parts of the Higher Self sent to Earth School, graduate with their energy glowing and illuminated by the knowledge they gathered at School. Other souls present their wisdom symbolically in a stack of books that detail their experiences. Many souls leave the Earth Campus metaphorically dragging a sack of stones that represents the energetic weight of their Classes. They seemed to go through School with a belief that the harder the life, the stronger the lesson. Those Beings that viewed life as a glorious gift might arrive with a symbolic basket of flowers, each petal representing a different occasion or event. Whether you graduate as a radiant soul or an exhausted spirit will depend on you and your choices.

Your Higher Self usually plans the length of time you are in School. However, that plan can change according to the choices you make and how the selections of other Students affect you. You have free will to react however you choose to every situation, but not the power to control the circumstance. Deciding to live in a healthy environment or a destructive one can affect the length of time your body is viable.

Many people cross over when their Higher Self had planned for them to do so. However, accidents can happen, and some lives can be shorter than what was expected. We are not controlled, as we have free will, but that fact can play a part in Students leaving the Earth Campus at a time when their soul did not plan.

If you end your School education earlier than expected, by taking your own life or by living in a self-destructive manner, you will most likely be disappointed when you get home. You cannot escape or bypass your lessons by ending your own life. Usually the returning spirits will continue to work on the same subjects they were attempting to learn in School, only in a different way. Usually, the soul will eventually choose to continue those lessons, one at a time, with the help of Angels and Guides. Additionally, they will have to work through the new lessons resulting from the surging energy created by their abrupt departure from Earth School. The people left behind can feel fear, confusion, self-doubt, anger, sorrow or deep emptiness. The departing soul's absence will be felt by many.

For many of you, your body will wear out as the human form deteriorates with time. Do not forget your body is a temporary sanctuary. Human bodies get weaker as they age. There are good reasons for that. When your eyes do not see as well as they did, you tend to look inside and examine what is there. Perhaps you slow down and see what you might have overlooked when you were physically stronger and moving faster. This time can offer an opportunity for you to review your life lessons and finish what has been left undone.

Getting old is a gift of extra time, so consider using it wisely by doing what can strengthen your Being. Even if your physical body wears out, your insight and inner fortitude can become stronger.

What each of you see and feel when you graduate from Earth School and leave your body will be unique to you. Let me stop here and share a few stories about the passage Students make when they return to their Higher Self.

Mia had traveled from Wisconsin to visit me. With her permission, I was shown the energy of guilt and sorrow surrounding her. Her father, Joe, who had recently crossed over, walked up to me wanting to help. He showed me that Mia had been taking care of him for several months before he crossed over, and had been determined to be with him when he left this earthly plane.

Mia had left his side for four or five minutes to use the bathroom, and when she returned, her father was gone. She felt devastated he had died alone and guilty because she had left him by himself.

Souls that have recently transitioned from the physical to the energetic form will often show me a movie of what happened. They can communicate most clearly this way.

Joe showed me Mia's living room. He lay on his hospital bed in one corner, and Mia sat by him holding his hand. He felt uncomfortable and in pain from cancer, but was still conscious of what was happening around him. When Mia left the room, he opened his eyes and watched his daughter walk away. He felt so grateful for the loving care she had shown him and felt she would find watching his transition hard. Joe's Higher Self stepped in and lifted his astral soul from his body. This was done as a gift to Mia, to save her the pain of watching her father's last breath. Joe's time in Earth School had lasted 87 years.

Then, Joe showed me his experience of crossing over. Once Joe had looked at Mia one last time, he quickly fell asleep. After a bit of time passed, he slowly woke up feeling something wet on his face. A dog was licking his cheek. His mother called to him from the kitchen telling him to hurry up, because breakfast was almost ready.

Joe threw back the covers and swung around to sit on the edge of his bed. He was in his childhood bedroom with his dog, Meatball. Joe had been eight years old the last time he had been in that room. He felt young, happy and full of energy.

His body had died while he was asleep, and his astral soul had crossed over into a place that let him know he had graduated from Earth School. He was overjoyed to see his mother and happily moved on.

Later, when he was ready, he reviewed what he had learned in his Classes in Tolerance, Dedication and Resilience. They had provided him with the opportunity to illuminate those parts of his Being, and he could now integrate those lessons into his Higher Self. He was also surprised he had learned lessons in Vulnerability and Integrity he had not planned. He called it extra credit.

Joe's soul energy is that of an Advisor. He has the gift to see both sides of a situation and the truth in-between. Presently, Joe gives advice to other Beings that ask for his help. He can give better counsel now, having gained considerable firsthand experience as a Student of Earth

School. He is content to remain just as he is for now, but has not ruled out learning more in the future.

Mia was comforted by her father's words that he left as a gift to her in our session. She realized that rather than experiencing death alone without her support, he had simply transformed and gone onto the next part of his soul journey in the company of those he loved.

A man from Western Nevada feared for the safety of his missing twenty-three-year-old brother, Sean, and called me for help in finding him. Asking for guidance, I was shown where they could find Sean's body, but his spirit had crossed over.

A few months later, I was able to meet with Sean's family and hoped that some of their questions about Sean's death would be answered. Sean showed me he had been so unhappy on Earth, he had decided to quit. Cocaine became his escape. Sean's depression became so deep and dark he could not see any reason to stay. He took his mother's gun, drove to the desert and ended his life.

As his body lay on the sand, his spirit rose up and went to what appeared to be a darkened room. His paternal grandfather was there for support, but not much was said. Sean saw a simple staircase at the far end of the room. Standing at the bottom of the stairs, looking up, he could barely make out a glass house filled with ferns and trees, vibrant with growth.

Some time passed, and he decided to move up on the first step. From there, he could see his mother back on Earth as she was told her son was gone. He watched her heart break. His understanding of loss and grief became deeper.

More time passed until he felt ready to take the second step. He saw the disappointment he had caused his brother and his friends. His understanding of responsibility became deeper. On and on he climbed, step by step, each one with something to teach him. He did not rush, but carefully considered each step before going to the next.

By the time he reached the last stair, nine Earth months had passed. Sean finally stood in front of the glass house. A man dressed in a simple white garment stood by the doorway. He asked Sean if he would like to come in and rest awhile. Sean agreed, curious to see what he would find.

Stepping into the house, Sean found himself on top of a grassy knoll. Through the glass ceiling, he could see the night sky overhead, a few scattered stars twinkling in the distance. He lay down on his back, put his hands behind his head and crossed his legs. His favorite music began to play and colored lasers flashed across the sky in rhythm to the beat. He was perfectly content. Sean stayed for many days.

When he felt stronger, he decided he was ready for more. First, he inherently knew to keep his astral soul separate from his Higher Self to prevent it from harming the whole of himself. His Guardian Angel and other

Helpers in the Light stood with him as he transitioned. Next, he and his Guardian Angel sat together in an energetic meadow with swaying green grass and clear blue skies overhead.

In the distance I could see a long line of Angels, each one holding just one thing. Every day in Earth School, Sean had hundreds of things to address, just as we all do – from taking care of his body to creating his life. The tasks had seemed never-ending to him. In this new setting, he would call one Angel forward, sit or walk with the Angel and deal with just one item. He and the Angels covered everything from life to suicide, and greed to generosity, until he was complete. The hundreds of Angels took their time with him, encouraging and supporting Sean through the entire process.

The last Angels held objects representing the energy created by his suicide—the unexpected change and ripple effect in the lives of the many Students on the Earth Campus who had been a part of his life. Eventually, Sean and his Guardian Angel were the only ones remaining in the meadow. Then he reached to his Higher Self and joined with the whole of himself to integrate what he had gathered.

Today, Sean helps other young people who are crossing over as a result of addiction or suicide. He takes his time, carefully listening to each soul's stories and concerns. He chose to become an example of what positive action can come from a shattering end, if you take responsibility and work at healing. He took the lessons from a devastating circumstance and began again as a more enlightened Being.

Whether you graduate feeling complete with your Classes or not, you can choose to continue your education or remain just as you are. It is your choice whether to stay on the levels of energy, come back to Earth School or seek wisdom in whatever way you select.

Your time in School has a beginning and an end. Everyone makes that transition. You might be curious to know what you will see and feel when you come home. As no two experiences are the same, know that yours will be unique to you. Do not fear the death of your body. It is not an ending, but rather a continuation of your soul journey.

On Earth, as a spirit in a human body, you gravitate toward certain environments to refresh and renew yourself when you feel stressed, confused or worn out. You might feel soothed sitting in silence on a boat dock with your feet dangling in the water. Or, you might find joy, surrounded by friends at a party, dancing and laughing.

Every spirit that graduates from Earth School has the same opportunity to be in a place of peace and comfort. If you feel fractured, defeated, scattered or just plain tired, there are souls dedicated to helping you. Their gift is to know the perfect combination of sound, color, texture or light that will resonate with your soul energy and vibration to calm, heal and strengthen you, just as they did for Sean. Other Beings that graduate choose to stay alone to contemplate the journey they just experienced.

In most cases, the first soul you see will be the one who fulfills three things for you. First, when you see this Being, you will know you have returned to your state of energy. Second, you are overjoyed to see the individual. Third, you trust them enough to lead you to where you are going. Some people even see an animal they loved when they were on the Earth Campus and happily move forward in the company of their long-missed pet. What helps you to be whole and strong will be different from what supports other souls.

Some Students believe the Creator will judge them when they return—that we are created from God, and He watches our every move and word. When we return home, these Students think we will stand in front of Him, and our life will be reviewed. If God is displeased with our actions in Earth School, He will cast us away forever. This can cause so much fear for some people that they hang onto life, refusing to let go until they have no option.

What I know to be true, is that we are created from the Light, which gives us life and free will to do whatever we want with our existence. We can decide to experience as many people, places and events as we desire. When we go home, we can share what we created as a result of our experience with other Beings who might benefit from our new knowledge.

The only judgment comes from your own soul, the whole of you, your Higher Self. Your Being will be pleased or ashamed by what you did or did not do. Many souls wish they had done a better job or paid closer attention to the true purpose of life, rather than the life lived solely for its physical aspects. A few who chose to be in chaos have added twisted and negative energy to their Higher Self by their actions and might dwell in shadow or darkness. They are usually left by themselves or joined by others on the same level.

The degree of your soul's illumination or shadow is evident, not only to you, but to every Being. Your essence belongs on the level of light or darkness it matches.

How will you judge your success? Are family, finances, wisdom, power, love, kindness or completed Classes the most important to you as you experience, learn and create on Campus? For each of you, the answers will be different. Truly feeling you did your best and learned from your mistakes, as well as your triumphs, is success.

While in Earth School, some teen-agers graduate high school with no future plans. You might see them hanging around their old campus, hoping to see friends and wasting time. In other words, they do not move on.

That can also happen with a soul. A small percentage of souls keep their energy on the Earth Campus, even after their body has expired. It can be painful for both the spirit and the Earth School Student who senses it. People on the Earth Campus might experience these Beings as ghosts, when in fact, they are spirits who did not move on. If those souls would choose to move into the Light their energy will come from a place of peace and greater understanding. There is more clarity in the Light. Most souls prefer this approach. They are able to continue their soul journey and learn to have a presence around their loved ones in a supportive, loving and encouraging manner.

⌒

Let's compare Soul Classes to high school classes. At the end of the fall term, receiving the grade of *C* in the subject of math on your report card would indicate you understood math, but still had not mastered parts of the subject material. Going into the winter term, you could choose to study harder, ask a teacher for help or hire a tutor. As you progressed, you might gain a better understanding of the basics that could pave the way to higher learning in college. Will you be satisfied with a *C*, knowing you will build on a weaker foundation than you would if you worked harder and achieved an *A*? The same is true for your Being.

Time and experience on the Earth Campus offer the opportunity to learn.

Perhaps my best advice to prime yourself for graduation and the journey beyond Earth School, is to live in the present, prepare for the future and be ready for anything. Know that no matter what takes place, you will continue.

Use this knowledge as the incentive to move forward with a stronger resolve. Altogether, it makes up the energy of your Higher Self.

- May your Earth Classes allow you to grow beyond what you believe you can accomplish.

- May you experience compassion and struggle, disappointment and kindness.

- May you find the grace to love and let go.

- May you stand strong when you feel lonely and face trials.

- May you have the courage and integrity to walk away when that choice is best.

- May you be satisfied, accomplish all you set out to do and return with additional wisdom you did not expect.

- May you be proud of both your accomplishments and the failures from which you learned.

- May you know you will be heard when you ask or pray, and have faith the answer will come at the right time.

- May all the things we have shared be of help and encourage you as you move forward.

- May you know that your future is bright and open and that opportunities and teachers await you.

- May you be blessed on every step of your journey.

In this moment, the Earth belongs to you. Cherish it, be gentle with it and be grateful for all it can teach you.

Now, Just Breathe

"Welcome To Earth School"

Glossary

Advisor - a soul born of the Counseling aspect of God

Advocate - a person who helps, acts and intercedes on behalf of someone who supports and takes action to assist an individual or community

Afterlife - continuing soul journey after the expiration of the human body

Angel - an extension of the Light of God with distinct purpose, form and function

Archangel - an Angel or Light Being projected from the Core Light of God

Astral Soul - a part or parts of the Higher Self that separate for the purpose of attending Earth School

Aura - the air or space surrounding a body with soul, an emanation of energy that encircles your Being

Being - the whole of your true self, soul, the fullness of your creation, essence, spirit, existence

Belief System - a formed belief of something, regardless of reality

Blessing - a gift of Divine Grace

Campus - the planet earth and all it contains, designed and created by the Creator

campus - a site on which the buildings of an organization or institution are located, built by people

Chakra - one of many points of physical or spiritual energy in and around the human body

Cherubim - Angels or Beings of Light who project from the Heart of God

Clairalience - the ability to clearly smell what exists on the energetic dimensions and is not present in the third dimension, the dimension of physical presence.

Clairaudient - the ability to hear inside your head without the use of physical ears

Clairgustance - the talent of perception that allows a person to taste a substance without putting something in his or her mouth, to perceive the essence of an element from the spiritual or ethereal realms through oral facilities

Clairsentient - the ability to sense within yourself the presence of energy, the knowing of what can only be felt and not seen with physical eyes

Clairvoyant - the ability to see with inner vision, without the use of physical eyes

Clarity - simple, clear perception

Class - lesson, circumstance, event from which to learn; everything that happens on the Earth Campus can be viewed as a class holding an opportunity to learn

Come Home - to have the body expire and the astral soul return to the levels of energy

Conduit - natural passage, flow area, pipe, duct, channel

Cosmic Gold - dimensional translucent energetic color consisting of all the colors in the Universe, with striations of glimmering gold woven throughout. Cosmic Gold transmutes the present energy into the most gracious for everyone.

Cosmic Silver - dimensional translucent energetic color. It holds all the colors in the Universe, with striations of glistening silver woven throughout. Cosmic Silver is used for soothing erratic energy.

Creative Energy - original, formative, inventive, imaginative, artistic energy of spiritual force

Creator - Higher Power, God, Goddess, the Oneness of Light, Originator

Creator Light - the Light of the Higher Power, the total of radiant, luminescent, glow, the Oneness of illumination

Creator Energy - the wholeness of all that is Love, a flowing of energy from God

Cross Over - when the astral soul leaves the expired human body and returns to the planes of energy

Dark - the absence of Light

Detractor - to diminish the importance, value, or effectiveness of

Dimension - a level of existence or consciousness

Distraction - interruption, diversion of focus, agitation

Divine - relating to, or directly of God

Earth Campus - the planet earth and all it contains, designed for the education of souls

Earth School - existing on the planet earth, created by God as a sacred place for souls to experience life, exercise their free will and create with their soul

Energetic Contracts - an agreement between two or more souls that define each soul's obligation under the circumstances outlined. That arrangement is required of you rather than exercising your free will as each opportunity presents itself.

Energetic Structure - configuration, formation, to shape from energy

Energetic Protection - to put safeguards in place, non-physical protection

Energy - vibrant quality, the ability of being active, a force, flowing through all people, vital and usable power

Energy Level - a plane of existence with distinct vibration

Energy Vibration - flowing pulsation of spiritual force

Enlighten - to furnish knowledge to, to give spiritual insight, inform, and make clear to

Existence - reality rather than appearance, the total of existent things, the actuality of being that is common to every form of being, life versus nothingness

Eyes of the Soul - inner vision or perception that is seen without the use of physical eyes

Faulty Thought - a thought, idea or opinion formed and held in the mind that is not based in reality

Foundation - a base upon which something stands or is supported, an underlying support, a body or ground upon which something is built up or overlaid

Free Will - voluntary choice or decision, freedom of humans to make choices that are not determined by prior causes or by Divine intervention

Feng-Shui - an ancient Chinese system of designing buildings and space arrangement according to special rules about the flow of energy, aimed at achieving harmony with the environment

Gift - a talent, or ability for doing something, often implies special favor by God or nature, suggests a marked natural ability that needs to be developed, inborn creative ability

Gift of Spirit - any talent or ability that is received from the Creator

Glimmer - to shine faintly or unsteadily, to give off a subdued unsteady reflection, to appear indistinctly with a faintly luminous quality

Grace - divine assistance given to humans for their regeneration or sanctification, a virtue coming from God, a state of sanctification enjoyed through divine grace, the thought or state of being considerate or thoughtful

God - Higher Power, the Supreme or Ultimate Reality, the Being perfect in power, wisdom and goodness who is worshiped as Creator and Ruler of the Universe

Graduation - the completion of Earth School education, when the astral soul leaves the expired body

Guardian - one assigned to protect or oversee another, the act or duty of protecting or defending

Guardian Angel - an Angel or Beam of Light who projects from the Creator for the purpose of supporting a single soul

Guide - one that leads or directs another's way, a person who exhibits and explains points of interest, someone that provides a person with guiding information

Guidance - the act or process of guiding, the direction provided by a guide, advice on vocational or educational problems given to students

Harmony - internal calm, tranquility, a blending of several into one tone

Herabim - an Angel or Beam of Light who projects from the Creator for the purpose of supporting a soul

Higher Light - elevated, above, superior, peak of illumination, the most positive force

Higher Self - the whole of one soul, the complete essence of self

Illumination – the action of illuminating or state of being illuminated, spiritual or intellectual enlightenment, lighting up

Illusion - misled, deception, a misleading image presented to the vision, something that deceives or misleads intellectually, perception of something objectively existing in such a way as to cause misinterpretation of its actual nature

Insight - the power or act of seeing into a situation, the act or result of capturing the inner nature of things or of seeing intuitively, discernment

Inner Vision - clairvoyance, to see without the use of physical eyes, to see with the vision of your soul

Inner Voice - clairaudient, to hear without the use of physical ears or auditory senses, to hear inside of yourself

Integrated - unified, blended, joined together

Integrity - firm adherence to a code of especially moral or artistic values, the quality or state of being complete or undivided

Intent - the act or fact of intending, the state of mind with which an act is done with a purpose

Intention - a determination to act in a certain way, resolve, what one intends to do or bring about, aim, object, goal one intends to accomplish or attain, settled determination, effort directed toward attaining or accomplishing, adds to these implications of effort directed toward attaining or accomplishing

Intuition - perception, insight, sixth sense, hunch, feeling, immediate recognition, the ability, or power of attaining

Judgment - the process of forming an opinion or evaluation by discerning and comparing, an opinion or estimate so formed, the capacity for judging, a proposition stating something believed or asserted

Knowing - to have knowledge of, to be acquainted or familiar with, to have experience of, to be aware of the truth or factuality of, be convinced or certain of, to have a practical understanding of

Life - the sequence of physical and mental experiences that make up the existence of an individual, one or more aspects of the process of living, spiritual existence transcending physical death, the period from birth to death, the form or pattern of something existing, in reality

Life Journey - life passage, travel, excursion during which time the soul is in the human body and on the Earth Campus

Light - a source of light: as a celestial body, spiritual illumination, inner light, enlightenment, truth, a particular illumination, something that enlightens or informs

Mental - relating to the mind, its activity, intellectual response of an individual, occurring or experienced in the mind, relating to spirit or idea in contrast to matter

Perfect Picture - a snapshot you carry in your mind that all else is measured by

Plane - a level of existence, consciousness, or development

Positive - constructive, fully assured, clear, constant, or certain in its action, characterized by affirmation, addition, inclusion, or presence rather than negation, having light and shade similar in tone to the tones of the original source of Light, having a good effect, favorable

Protective Aura - to place protection in and around the space that surrounds your body or soul, an emanation of shielding light energy and color

Purpose - something set up as an object or end to be attained, intended goal

Relationship Aura - an egg-shaped energy held between two people that holds the energy created within the relationship.

Sacred - devoted exclusively to one service or use (as of a person or purpose), entitled to reverence and respect

school - an organization or institution that provides instruction for teaching

School - existing on the planet Earth, created by God as a sacred place for souls to experience life, exercise their free will and create with their soul

Self-Discovery - the act or process of achieving self-knowledge

Seraphim - an Angel or Being of Light, who projects from the Creator for the purpose of carrying information between other Angels or souls

Shadow - gloom, shade, dimness, a place or space that is obscured from light

Society - association with other people, a social group whose members have developed organized patterns of relationships through interaction with one another, a community, nation, or broad grouping of people having common traditions, institutions, and collective activities and interests, a part of a community that is a unit distinguishable by particular goals or standards of living or conduct

Society's Expectation - preconceived expectations concerning behavior, such as morals, ethics, values, acceptable ways of living as defined by a culture, populace, or people of like ethics and morals

Soul - an individual spark of energy originating from the Creator, the accumulation of experience and energy and original spark of essence actuating cause of an individual life, the spiritual energy embodied in human beings, a person's total self, eternal, spiritual or force, an active or essential part of existence.

Soul-Body Connection - the partnership between body and soul that allows the soul to be participating in Earth School

Soul Group - a "grouping" of souls born of the same aspect of the Creator

Soul Growth - the eternal energy of each individual in the process of increasing or expanding

Soul Journey - the process of movement, experience, actions, and existence of the eternal energy of each individual, from the moment of a Being's creation throughout eternity

Spirit - soul, inner self, life force, Chi, essence, Being

Spirit Guide - a soul, without a human body, that helps to guide another soul or souls that are in the human body and in Earth School

Spiritual Level - a plane of existence, where vibration and energy is distinct, where soul is without body

Stained - to suffuse with color, to bring discredit on, to discolor

Steadfast - firmly fixed in place, immovable, not subject to change, firm in belief, determination, or adherence, loyal, faithful

Telepathic - the ability to communicate directly from one person's mind to another's without speech, writing, or other signs or symbols

Third Dimension - thickness, depth, or apparent thickness or depth that confers solidity on an object, a quality that confers reality

Thrive - flourish, true learning to grow vigorously, prosper, to progress toward or realize a goal despite or because of circumstances

Thought Form - an idea, concept, belief, opinion or philosophy that takes shape in the human mind and is believed regardless of truth or reality

Tool - implement, instrument, device, means, or apparatus used as a means of achieving something

Toxic - containing or being poisonous material, especially when capable of causing death or serious debilitation, extremely harsh, malicious, harmful, sarcasm

True Self - the whole of a soul without foreign energy, a soul that is free of outside input, persuasion, or interference

Truth - the state of being the case, fact, the body of real things, events, and facts, actuality, transcendent fundamental or spiritual reality

Unity of Souls - Oneness of all souls, the connection of all souls

Universal Understanding - what is known and understood, mutual comprehension

Universe - the total of all matter and energy, creation, the entire celestial cosmos

Vibration - an instance of vibration, vacillation, emanation, aura, or spirit that infuses or vitalizes someone or something and that can be instinctively sensed or experienced, a distinctive usually vibrant atmosphere capable of being sensed

Vision - sight, the act or power of seeing using physical eyes or the inner vision of the soul, emanation, aura, or a gift of discernment or foresight, direct mystical awareness of energy

Voices that do not Belong - a voice that is heard from without or within a person that clouds the truth, belittles, or distracts you

Author's contact information:

Catherine Adams

Welcome to Earth School

P.O. Box 833

Seymour, TN 37876

Email Catherine directly at:

Welcometoearthschool@yahoo.com

Visit the website at:

www.Welcometoearthschool.com